The painting on the cover, And the Word Became Flesh, *is by Indian Christian artist Frank Wesley, who draws inspiration from Hindu culture to present Christian truths in striking and fresh ways. The colour of the painting develops from the blue lotus flower, symbol of purity and divinity, into pink for joy and to the pale golden light of spiritual wisdom (also seen on the child's forehead). The design emphasizes oval shapes, suggesting an egg, symbol of life before birth.*

D1461853

Published by
The Bible Reading Fellowship
First Floor, Elsfield Hall
15–17 Elsfield Way, Oxford OX2 8FG

ISBN 1 84101 184 3
First published 2004
10 9 8 7 6 5 4 3 2 1 0

Acknowledgments
Unless otherwise stated, scripture quotations are taken from the Holy
Bible, New International Version, copyright © 1973, 1978, 1984 by
International Bible Society, and are used by permission of Hodder &
Stoughton Limited. All rights reserved. 'NIV' is a registered trademark
of International Bible Society. UK trademark number 1448790.

A catalogue record for this book is available from the British Library

Printed and bound in Great Britain by
Bookmarque, Croydon

CLAIRE DISBREY

...AND THE WORD BECAME FLESH AND LIVED AMONG US

JOHN 1:14

LISTENING TO PEOPLE OF OTHER FAITHS

ACKNOWLEDGMENTS

I would like to thank the members of the many different faith communities who made this book possible—especially the people who talked to me and gave me not just their time but, in a real sense, themselves, as they shared their experiences, their thoughts and feelings. Thanks also to all the others who gave me suggestions and introductions, set up visits and interviews, welcomed me and showed me around. Sue White helped me with some typing when things got hectic, Dr Hugh Beatie, a colleague from the Open University, helped me with the preparation of Chapter 5, and Canon David Winter, a long-standing friend, supported, encouraged and advised me from the beginning of this project through to its completion.

CONTENTS

FOREWORD

This is a book by a Christian, for Christians, but about the other major world religions. For once, however, the members of those faiths are allowed to speak for themselves, so that the reader is given an unusual opportunity to see and sense both the common ground of religious experience that we all share and also the distinctions of belief that keep us apart. The author's hope is that from such a sharing we may learn to respect the deep wellsprings of divinity wherever they appear, and also be in a better position to speak to those of other faiths about the Christian faith that moulds and shapes our own beliefs.

Claire Disbrey is emphatically not a syncretist. She does not believe that 'we all believe in the same God, don't we?' Neither is she a minimalist, trying to find the vestiges of some lowest common denominator on which all religious people could agree. She seems to be happiest with an inclusive stance (as distinct from an exclusive one), looking for the experiences of prayer, worship, grace, salvation, hope and trust that mark the faith journeys of men and women across the religious divides. In this approach she stands with the apostle Paul as he addressed the Areopagus in Athens, starting with the shared experience of creation, human life and the religious spirit before moving on to the distinctive elements of his own faith as a Christian.

In the last few years we have all become aware that we can't any longer live our lives in religious and cultural space capsules. We share the planet—and even our own small islands—with people whose worldview is radically different from ours. Many of them despise the materialism and godlessness of the West, which they tend to equate with 'Christianity'. Christians themselves are increasingly aware that they live alongside people whose religious beliefs and practice are at least as committed and fervent as their own, and sometimes notably more so. Relating to those people and their communities is not only a wise course from the point of view of social harmony, but a Christian privilege. That was how Paul saw his mission to the 'Gentiles'—the sophisticated Greek culture and also the people in what he called the 'regions beyond'. He longed to share with them the 'mystery' of God's revelation in Christ, but he did it not from a position of ignorance or scorn of their beliefs but from respect for them as people made in God's image, with the priceless human gifts of conscience and moral choice.

This book is a challenging and in some ways disturbing read for Christians. It asks us to rethink our understanding of those who have found spiritual fulfilment and a serene faith without embracing the Christian revelation. But it also offers us a way to be 'witnesses' to Christ to them, not driven to silence by the sincerity of others but set free to share with them the fulfilment, serenity and freedom that we have found through our own encounter with the One who is 'our way, our truth, our life'.

David Winter

WHY WE NEED TO LISTEN
TO PEOPLE OF OTHER FAITHS

INTRODUCTION

In my experience some Christians are getting uneasy about the way they talk about Jesus.

Before we had friends and colleagues who were practising Hindus, Muslims and Sikhs, it seemed quite easy to say that only Christians knew the truth about what God is like and how to find him, that only Christians could talk to God in prayer and feel confident that he listens to them, that only Christians had an inner power to overcome their naturally selfish natures.

Before we began to see almost daily in the news the awful results of people believing that they have exclusive rights to divine revelation, truth and righteousness, it seemed quite easy to say that God had revealed himself only through Jesus, that we must go out to people of other religions and do all that we can to make them into Christian disciples and so save them from the consequences of their sins.

For many Christians in the West, however, the world has changed, leaving us with ambiguous loyalties and sometimes an uncomfortable two-facedness in what we feel happy to say in different contexts. Some of our churches are telling us that we must hold on to the fact that our religion is unique and exclusive, while neighbours and friends are saying that the only hope for world peace is that people give up exclusive claims about their religion and accept that they are not the only ones who are right. Tolerance and respect of other people's beliefs and cultures have become the new virtues in today's world, but many of us feel equally uneasy about the idea that truth in religion is relative or that all religions lead us, by different routes, to the same God. We do want to echo the words of Charles Wesley (1708–88) in the hymn 'Jesus, the name high over all'—'Oh that the world might taste and see the riches of his grace, the arms of love that compass me, would all mankind embrace'—but we are starting to lose confidence in our ability to help this happen.

In this book I want to explore this dilemma and help Christians from all sorts of backgrounds to work through it in their own way, not with a deep biblical or theological discussion of the exclusive claims of Christianity, although my aim is to be faithful both to the Bible and to orthodox Christian teaching; not by philosophical arguments about the nature of truth, and not by detailed analyses of the official beliefs and practices of other religions—all these can be found elsewhere. I want to encourage Christians to look at some facts about today's world and give them a chance to listen to what ordinary British people who follow other faiths say about what their religion means to them— what they think is unique about their experience of God, of prayer and worship and ethical living. In doing so, I believe we shall find that some of the things Christians say are factually untrue, some are a crude distortion of what the Bible as a whole teaches, and some will inevitably come across as too arrogant and dogmatic to open up any sort of helpful discussion.

CONVERSATIONS

Living as I do in North London, it has not been hard to find people who are enthusiastic about their faith and happy to share their thoughts and feelings with me. The central section of this book will be a series of extracts from these conversations. My hope is that these alone will be a substantial help to Christians in finding a confident and comfortable way of talking about their God and Saviour, a way that as well as commending him as effectively as possible, can also, in our multi-faith world, 'make for peace and build up our common life'.[1]

It would only be fair to warn you at this stage that although I had some expectations of what I would hear, these conversations moved me, and stimulated and changed my thinking in ways I had not foreseen.

Before we look at the conversations, however, it will help to look at the sorts of things Christians say about people of other faiths and to think through our reactions to these things. Do we perhaps feel an uncomfortable tension between what we think we *ought* to say and what we feel we *want* to say, to and about our friends, our colleagues, our partners? Are we unclear how these opinions have been reached, or what passages from the Bible have been used to reach them? Do we feel unsettled by the attempts of some contemporary theologians to resolve this tension?

We then need to look at how the world is changing as we move into the 21st century and to answer the question of why, particularly now, we need to open up this subject. What are modernity, globalization and plurality? How have they changed ordinary people's perceptions of the world, their ideas about faith and truth? In what different ways have religious people been responding to these changes?

One of the ways we need to change our perception is to look at our own religion, not as the only religion there is, or the only one we need to consider, but as one religion among many. Over several years of teaching Religious Studies to adult students, I have seen how this change of perspective can be quite hard for some people, but can enlarge our understanding of and our commitment to our own religion, making our conversations with people of other faiths both more informed and more effective. Studying other religions in this way opens our eyes to the enormous diversity of beliefs and practices that can be found under the broad headings of Buddhism, Judaism and so on. This perception is very usefully turned back on to our own religion, so that we come to realize that our way of looking at Jesus, what he has done and how we need to respond to him is very different from the way some other groups, and maybe the majority, of Christians understand him.

After reading the conversations, we will return to the question of talking about Jesus in today's world, look again at the challenge to do it and consider some suggestions for the way to go about it.

CHAPTER 1

WHAT CHRISTIANS SAY ABOUT PEOPLE OF OTHER FAITHS

Since starting to teach undergraduates about the six main world religions, I find my ears attuned to remarks made casually in conversations around the kitchen table, in Bible studies, sermons and books of all kinds, that reveal what Christians think about people of other faiths. Some of these remarks are the result of careful study of the Bible or other philosophical deliberations; others have been picked up in all sorts of places and are made for all sorts of reasons.

THE UNIQUENESS OF CHRISTIANITY

Among these remarks, there are some that make claims about the uniqueness and exclusiveness of the Christian religion. While it is clear that all religions are unique in some ways, I find that some of these claims are just factually untrue, some are very selective in their use of the Bible and many come over as embarrassingly superior and dismissive. Here is a sample of them. You might like to consider which of these claims you think at the moment are factually accurate and unambiguously taught in the Bible, and which you would feel comfortable expressing in the company of your fellow believers *and* in the company of friends and colleagues from other faith communities.

- Christianity is unique among the world's religions because:
  - it's about God revealing himself to us, rather than people trying to work it out for themselves;
  - it's about God coming to earth in human form;
  - it's about being saved by grace rather than by our own effort.
- God has only revealed himself through the early Jewish and Christian religions—his covenant people and his Church. Other claims to revelation are mistaken.
- God has only come to the earth in Jesus. Claims that other people have been 'God with us' are wrong.
- Jesus is the only way to God. People who don't approach God through Jesus can neither know him nor experience his presence in their lives.
- Only Christians can really meet God in prayer and have confidence that he hears and answers them.
- The God Christians worship is the only real God; followers of other religions worship false gods. It would therefore be wrong for a Christian to be present at, or take part in, the worship of another religion.
- Jesus is the only acceptable sacrifice, able to open the way to heaven for those who follow him. If people haven't heard about Jesus and consciously accepted his offer to save them, God can't forgive their sins and they can't have a relationship with him or go to heaven.
- Christian baptism is the only way to become a member of God's saved community.

TRUTH AND RELATIVISM

One way to get around the problem of what to think about other faiths is to take a particular view about the importance of truth in religion—either that there isn't any or that it doesn't matter. The word 'relativism' is often used in this context. Some Christians say things that express this idea, others reject it. You might like to pick from the statements below the one you think is nearest to your point of view.

- All religions are basically saying the same thing.
- Even if the path is different in other religions, the goal is the same.
- We should respect everyone's beliefs, because all religions help people to live better lives and that's what is really important.
- It doesn't matter what religious beliefs you hold because there's no real, objective truth in any of it. Religious truth is a different sort of truth; the whole idea of being right and wrong doesn't apply in religions.
- It's wrong to try to change someone else's religion because it can destroy their culture and identity, and those values are more important than truth.
- In many ways God is a mystery to us all. We can't pin him down with words. No religion has complete access to 'the ultimate truth' about God.
- Sincerity of faith or devotion can't save you if you are sincerely wrong or devoted to the wrong thing.
- If I am right in what I believe (as I think I am) then anyone who believes anything else must be wrong.

A MORE INCLUSIVE RELIGION?

Theologians, biblical specialists and philosophers from many different backgrounds have worked to try to make Christianity into a more inclusive religion. Here are some of the things they say. Do you feel you could go along with some of these comments?

- There is one God who is there: people all over the world are trying to find him.
- God's Spirit is active all over his world, showing people what he is like, drawing people into a relationship with him and bringing his salvation to them.

- Most religions have their insights and errors and can be used for good or bad ends; no one is right about everything.
- Jesus' death on the cross 'for the sins of the whole world' is not much of a victory if only a tiny minority of the human race is saved by it.
- The possibility of being saved must, from simple justice, be accessible to everyone. It's not fair if God's salvation is limited by where you are born or by the disobedience and ineffectiveness of the Church.
- The great monotheistic, ethical religions of the world don't come in the same category as the immoral, pagan religions of Bible times.
- Religions don't save anyone: God does. Everyone who is saved will be saved by the grace of God alone. While we seem to want to exclude people from this grace, God wants to include everyone.
- Jesus' sacrifice for sin means that anyone who believes and trusts in God's grace can (like the Old Testament saints) be forgiven whether they have heard about Jesus or not.
- If you have discovered that being a Christian has made it possible for you to find God, it is neither arrogant nor intolerant to recommend it to someone else.
- The only hope for world peace is that people give up exclusive claims about their own religion and accept that they are not the only ones who are right.

You might find it interesting to come back to this list of the things that Christians say when you have listened to the people talking about their beliefs, values and experiences in the rest of this book, and see if you have changed your mind about what you want to say about people of other faiths and how you want to talk to your friends and neighbours about Jesus.

CHAPTER 2

THE CHANGING WORLD

Many people in Britain began to notice that the world was changing in the 1960s. David Lodge, in an amusing novel about a group of Roman Catholic university students living through this period, put it like this: 'At some point in the nineteen-sixties, Hell disappeared. No one could say for certain when this happened. First it was there, then it wasn't... On the whole the disappearance of Hell was a great relief, though it brought new problems.'[2]

Of course, people's awareness of what was going on depended on the circumstances of their lives at that time. I was pregnant for most of the '60s, but I still made myself a pair of hot pants, got hold of a Beatles wig to entertain the youth group and read a copy of *Lady Chatterley's Lover* hidden in a brown paper cover.

Through the '60s in Britain, a series of Acts of Parliament removed what Christians thought of as 'sins' from the category of crimes: theatrical and literary censorship was relaxed; homosexual acts, abortion and divorce became matters of private conscience rather than state control; and a Commonwealth Immigration Act changed the pattern of immigration into the country. All around the world, students began to revolt against authority, by growing their hair and organizing protest marches and 'sit-ins'; the Vietnam War began, CND started campaigning against nuclear weapons, and the IRA asserted its demand for a united Ireland in earnest. Since then the changes have accelerated. Who could have predicted how different our lives would be in the 21st century, after the rise of feminism, the fall of Communism, the Iranian and the IT revolutions?

Even from the early days, the response of religious people to these changes varied enormously. In 1963 an Anglican bishop wrote a book called *Honest to God*, which had a chapter entitled 'Christian Freedom in a Permissive Society'. The bishop argued that the world was becoming such a different place that the most fundamental categories of our theology and morality 'must go into the melting pot'.[3] Not long afterwards, an Anglican woman called Mary Whitehouse started an organization, that later blossomed into 'The Nationwide Festival of Light', to try to preserve the Christian values that seemed to many to be slipping away on the raft of change.

There is a whole range of contrasting ways of dealing with the question about how far, if at all, religions need to change if they are going to survive changes in the cultures that surround them. You can see this contrast in the way people feel about bringing the language of Bible translations and worship up to date. Some think that young Christians should learn Elizabethan English; others that everything should be rewritten so that it conforms to modern ideas of political correctness. This is often characterized as a divide between liberals and conservatives, but it is of course more complicated than that. People look in many different directions to answer the question about what it's right to believe and to do. We'll be thinking later about the different responses religious people have made to the way the world has changed, but first we'll look more closely at what has happened.

Social commentators have coined words like 'modernity', 'globalization', 'plurality' and 'secularization' to talk about the changing world, and while there are many disputes about what these words mean, or how far they apply, they are a helpful way of thinking about it.

MODERNITY

The word 'modernity' is used for a particular way of thinking about the world and our place in it that began in Western Europe in the

17th century. People connect its beginnings with the work of the French philosopher René Descartes (1596–1650), who asked the question, 'How can I be certain of anything?' He came up with the answer that the only thing he knew for sure was, in the now famous Latin phrase, *cogito ergo sum*—'I think, therefore I am.' This shifted God from the centre of people's thinking and developed into faith in the ability of ordinary people to reason things out for themselves —belief in rationality as a universal attribute of all but the most dysfunctional human beings and the answer to all humanity's questions and problems.

Although it wasn't clearly recognized as such at the time, there are important ways in which modernity is antagonistic to religion, or at least to the dogmatic, authoritarian, supernatural religion that dominated Western Europe at the time. As modernity developed and spread and proved so practically successful as a worldview, and secularists grew impatient with the churches' apparent determination to suppress it, fight it or ignore it as irrelevant, the question was increasingly asked: can religions survive in the modern world? The answer often given was, 'No'. But people had not counted on the many different forms that religions can take, the different roles they can play in a society and their ability to change dramatically while still holding on to their roots and special identities.

Science, industrial technology and later the technology of communication took off. Rational rather than religious bases were found for ethics, government, education and economics, which then became ruled by secular rather than religious values—ideas about human rights and individual autonomy, tolerance, equality of opportunity and democracy. Perhaps the four most influential social novelties that emerged in the modern world were industrialization, urbanization, occupational specialization and mass education. The economic base it favoured was capitalism and, in terms of politics, the idea of democratic nation states. Perhaps the most pervasive emotion was a restless and still unsatisfied search for certainty.

GLOBALIZATION

'Globalization' is the word that has been used to describe the way this rationalist philosophy and way of life, which developed in Western Europe, has been spreading all around the world. It could equally well be described as the modernization or Westernization (some call it the Americanization) of the world. The first photograph of the earth taken from space was published in *Life* magazine in the 1960s. From that distance, it looked almost as though it could be taken in someone's hand. It was not long before you could fax a message to almost every capital city in the world, fly to one of them in just a few hours, buy a McDonald's burger and some Marks and Spencer's underwear, and e-mail a note home to say 'Wish you were here!' It was not long before the real power in economics and politics was wielded not by nation states but by multi-national corporations and inter-political alliances. It was not long before the actions and reactions of people groups had to be made in the limelight of global media interest and comment, and were judged by the standards of Western, secular values.

Migration from the countryside to the town grew into migration from anywhere to anywhere—Britons living in South America, Arabs working in France, Asians settling in Britain, Africans studying in America, Americans moving to Israel. For some people, this means a new freedom: one of my sons presently lives in Greece and one in Spain, and both enjoy the difference, especially in the weather. For others, however, it means even more insecurity as they feel their communities being undermined and their national and cultural identity (some only recently liberated from Western colonialism) being eroded again.

To understand more about these feelings of uncertainty and insecurity that so characterize the contemporary world, we need to explore the idea of plurality.

PLURALITY

In medieval Europe there was one Church, one empire, one world-view. People knew what was right to believe about everything because the Church told them, and everyone around them believed the same. Anyone who dissented was judged seriously maladjusted and dangerous.

The Reformation changed that. From the middle of the 16th century there were two great religious movements—the recently revived Roman Catholic Church setting out with confidence to evangelize the world, and a growing number of Protestant churches who, although they all took the Bible seriously, could not agree on how to interpret it. For example, Zwingli and Luther disagreed about the meaning of the Holy Communion service; Calvin and Arminius disagreed about predestination.

Rational debate, with the best will in the world, did not seem able to resolve these differences. Years of wars, killings and executions did not resolve them either. In 1648, 30 years of religious war that had almost brought Western Europe to a standstill were declared a 'no-score draw'. Western Europeans were forced to accept the fact that people believe different things about God, about what Jesus has done, about the nature of the Church, and about how to interpret the Bible's moral teaching, and the only way forward was for them to get on, to live peaceably side by side.

Travel, for evangelism, trade, empire-building, and for leisure, brought home the fact that there were sophisticated and successful cultures in other parts of the world that did not recognize the Christian God at all, or find any need for the idea of him. The Christian way of looking at the world, divided as it was over the details, appeared as only one of an amazing selection of alternatives, and, as travel and migration boomed, that fact came closer and closer to home.

This is the fact of plurality. It can be an uncomfortable fact to live with. It raises problems with our ideas about truth and the strong attraction some of us have to feeling certain that we are right. Some people will go to great lengths to avoid facing up to it or exposing their children to it. They would rather their children were brought up thinking that everyone in the world shares their beliefs and values, their way of looking at the world.

I myself used to use the description 'unbelievers' to talk about people who were not Christians, but I see now that this reveals a myopic viewpoint. I was taken to task quite angrily by a secularist colleague who asked me not to call him an unbeliever. 'I believe as many things as you, as passionately as you,' he told me. 'It's just that they are different things.'

Before we look at some of the different ways religious people have responded to the changing world, we need to ask one more question about it.

SECULARIZATION

Were those people right who predicted that the world would become an increasingly secular place, that religion would die out in the face of the success of rationalism and science? Some people think the jury is still out on this question, but the majority of those who study modern societies are coming round to a resounding, if provisional, 'No'. Certainly, science is seen to have more predictable explanations of why things happen, and institutional Christianity is declining in Western Europe, although you can still find pockets of vitality and growth. Western cultures are becoming more pluralistic and our states increasingly neutral on the matter of religion. Religion may be backing out of public life in Britain and becoming a marginal, private option, but we must beware of thinking that the forms of religion we know are the only forms that religions can take, or of projecting what has happened in Britain on to the rest of the world.

In other parts of the world, particularly in the East, science and technology are not seen to be antagonistic to religions. The USA has had a pluralistic population and a neutral state since its foundation but is still, in terms of attendance at worship, a remarkably religious society. In Britain, institutional religion may have lost most of its social significance but this does not mean that people's search for answers to religious questions and ways of expressing them have disappeared. We only have to remember the way people responded to the death of Diana, Princess of Wales, in 1997 to confirm this. In other parts of the world, religion is coming back on to the political agenda—Christianity in Brazil, Islam in Iran and Egypt, Hinduism in India.

Neither does plurality necessarily weaken the plausibility of religion as a way of looking at the world. The amazing rise of the strange ideas and practices that we class together as the New Age movement shows that the idea of a supermarket of religions that people can mix and match to suit their own inclinations is probably going to be an attractive one to Western Europeans in the 21st century.

POSTMODERNITY

What may be becoming clear is that now, in the 21st century, people are moving on from modernity. That question about certainty, which rationality seemed for a time to answer, never really went away. People have now become disillusioned with the idea that human rationality, science and technology can produce all the answers we need or solve all our problems. They can show us how to make dynamite, nuclear energy and designer babies, but not how to stop people using them in a selfish, destructive way. They can show us how to make the lives of wealthy populations secure and comfortable but not how to get people to share the good things of the earth or preserve them for future generations.

The enduring, persistent problem of plurality makes it seem unlikely that there is one overarching story, one objective truth about how the world is and how we should live in it. A new, rather devastating answer has emerged to Descartes' old question: 'How can I be certain of anything?' It is that you can't be. Human beings now must learn to live with uncertainty, to live peaceably side by side with people who believe different things from themselves and find whatever way they can of making sense of it all. One cynic has proposed that the slogan of postmodernity should be *Tesco ergo sum*—'I shop, therefore I am'!

Plurality, the fact that people hold different worldviews, that they look at the world from different perspectives, has slipped into pluralism—the idea that all forms of belief and lifestyles are equally 'true' and valid.

This is the challenge to Christians in the 21st century. How are we, as people committed to an old story, an ancient tradition based on faith in an objective, living God who has revealed himself to us in Jesus Christ, going to respond to this new world? In our next chapter we will look at some of the options.

CHAPTER 3

HOW RELIGIONS HAVE RESPONDED TO THE CHANGING WORLD

There was a good chess club in the village before the railway came. It met on winter Tuesday evenings at 6 o'clock. Ties and suits were the order of the day. A small self-appointed committee arranged the tables and decided who would play with whom.

As the commuters moved in and the village grew, the chess club boomed, but there were soon calls for change. Eight o'clock would be more suitable for those travelling home from town; Friday would be a more popular day; and why not meet all through the year? People started turning up in jeans, asking if they could play with their friends and murmuring about wanting an elected committee. Strong words were used at the annual meeting; angry letters appeared in the village magazine. Eventually the club split: half continued to meet on winter Tuesdays in the village hall and the other half on Friday evenings in a back room at the pub.

The village hall club wrote a constitution, setting out such things as how the committee was chosen, their role and authority, where and when the club met, a dress code, what was served as refreshments (it was always ham sandwiches and tea) and how the tables were to be set out. This document was displayed each week next to a book about the rules of chess, and both were often referred to. When people brought in fancy moves they had seen in international competitions, they were told that if it was in the rule book they could do it, if it wasn't they couldn't—no discussion.

The committee made it quite clear that newcomers to the village were most welcome, but asked them, if they wanted to become regular members, to sign a form saying that they accepted the rule book, the constitution and the authority of the committee. When someone suggested they could get more people in if they rearranged the tables, they were told that the placing of the tables was written into the constitution. When a Jewish couple wanted to join, they were told that only ham sandwiches had ever been served at the chess club; it was their tradition. When someone complained that the boards were getting tatty and some of the pieces were chipped, the committee said they had been used by their fathers and their fathers before them. When the village hall began to fall down and the heating failed, the committee turned down an offer to use the school, shored up the hall with boards and tarpaulins and brought in paraffin heaters. Gradually numbers began to fall.

The new club that was set up in the back room of the pub flourished. They served beer and bar snacks and people could come in and go out when they liked and choose with whom they played. In fact, they could agree their own rules as they went along if they liked. When someone suggested that they install some computers to play against, it was hailed as a great innovation—and if they wanted to play *Tomb Raider* instead, that was fine too. When new people said that chess was really rather a difficult game to learn and each game took too long to reach a conclusion, a democratic decision was made to make the boards smaller and give up the knights—always tricky movers! Eventually most of the players gave up on the character pieces altogether and started playing a complicated sort of draughts.

Some years later, when some new people moved in and asked if there was a chess club in the village, they were told that two old men used to play occasionally on a Tuesday night in the ruins of the village hall, until last year when one of them died, and there was a very popular club, called 'The New Chess Club', that met in a back room of the pub on Friday nights, but they didn't play chess any more.

CHANGING TOO LITTLE AND CHANGING TOO MUCH

This is the dilemma that faces religions in a changing world. There are, of course, big differences between sports clubs and religious communities, but in both, when things are changing all around them, not to change at all is one way of dying, and changing too much is another.

In today's fragmented world, religions are just one part of the way culture is expressed in a society. Other ways of expressing it can change independently, so that a religion can find itself at odds with the prevailing culture in which it is embedded. As an example of this, one effect of globalization is that the idea of 'human rights' is to a large extent becoming the universal ethic of our world. It is, however, an ethic that comes out of Western secularism, and the view that a whole ethical system can be based on the rights of individuals sits very uneasily with the world's religions, which are widely concerned with conquering self-centredness rather than putting it centre stage, with the needs of the community rather than the individual and, many of them, with obedience to the revelation of a sovereign, creator God.

As some Muslims argue, if you believe in a sovereign God who has revealed to his creatures how they should live, the idea that ethics can be based solely on the rights of human beings seems quite extraordinary. The fact that churches and other religious groups in the European Union have been allowed to slip out of equal opportunity legislation and close jobs to people solely on the grounds of their gender or sexual orientation brings this clash between subcultures starkly out in the open.

Christians are divided on how the Church should respond. Some feel that it should not let the secular world set its agenda. I heard this view expressed strongly in the General Synod of the Church of England at around the time a cartoon appeared in a national newspaper depicting the 'Grim Reaper'—a symbol of death—comforting an Anglican bishop, sitting weeping as his church disintegrated around him. 'There, there,' the Reaper was saying, 'you don't have to change if you don't want to.'

Just in the way that the railway's arrival in agricultural villages produced dramatic changes and brought difficult decisions to the lives of the inhabitants, so has the arrival of modernity, and now postmodernity, to the religious communities of the world. These changes can be seen both as threatening a settled way of life, and as opening up exciting new opportunities and challenges. The difficult question is about how far you can go in adapting to these changes, so that your community remains relevant and viable without losing touch with the roots and traditions that make it distinctive and worthwhile. It is possible to separate out four ways that people can respond to these sorts of changes, although in real life they merge and mingle in complicated ways.

ISOLATION

A religious community can isolate itself from the rest of the culture, retreat into a ghetto where the members continue their chosen way of life, and at the same time become increasingly irrelevant and strange to people outside. Traditions of distinctive dress and rules about contact with non-members and use of the media may be set up. There has always been a tradition in East and West of withdrawing from the social world in order to pursue the spiritual one, and groups like the Amish communities in America, or the Luba-vitch (ultra-Orthodox) Jewish communities that can be found in the London areas of Stamford Hill or Golders Green, or some of the Exclusive Christian Brethren, have found this a continuingly viable way of being religious in the contemporary world. People living in these sorts of communities are, to a large extent, shielded from the intellectual and practical questions that plurality raises.

DEFENCE

Other communities can go on the offensive, aggressively defending conservative beliefs and traditions. This is the response that, at its extreme, has been labeled 'fundamentalism', but this emotive word needs some unpacking. It originated as a description for a particular view towards the Bible that emerged in early 20th-century America, but has become a word to describe a particular kind of response to the assaults of the modern world. As a way of using the Bible, fundamentalism insists that every part of it be taken literally and applied uncompromisingly. It came to the fore in the 1920s in the United States, specifically as a response to modernity—to a liberal theology that seemed to be giving more authority to human reason than the 'plain teaching' of the Bible, and to the secularization of society and its values. G.M. Marsden, in the *New Dictionary of Theology*[4] describes a fundamentalist as a 'militantly anti-modernist evangelical'. As a reaction to unsettling changes in the culture around them, feeling their beliefs and their way of life under threat, fundamentalists simplify and harden what they believe to be the essentials —the fundamentals—of their belief and practice. They lay down not only the way scripture must be approached but also how it is to be interpreted and applied. They are keen to 'hold the line', to make the interpretations and applications of yesterday the only sound and acceptable ones, often picking specific areas of dispute and making attitudes to them determinative of authentic faith.

Fundamentalists take positive action—sometimes aggressive, sometimes violent action—to try to maintain the conditions necessary for their beliefs to survive. This will include attacking other members of their own faith, accusing them of undermining or destroying it by their willingness to reassess or change things. Christian anti-abortion groups in America who attack clinics and threaten the people who work in them, ultra-Orthodox Jews who stone Sabbath breakers in Israel, the anti-gay lobby in the Church of England who obstruct appointments and refuse to accept the oversight of their bishops, and Muslims who try to impose their version of Shari'ah law on unwilling communities, are some extreme examples of this sort of defensive response to modernity.

Fundamentalists tend to be those who strongly assert the uniqueness and exclusiveness not only of their own faith, but of their own version of it—the group of people they can affirm and work with often getting smaller and smaller as other members of their faith communities adapt to the changes going on around them.

The word 'fundamentalist' has also recently been used in a rather different way for groups of people who, feeling that their identity is being undermined by the globalization process, rally around a religious label to fight for what they see as the survival of their way of life. The militant postures taken by some Muslim groups towards the West can be seen in this light, as can the Hindu nationalistic movement in India and the unrest in Sri-Lanka. This resurgence of religion into the political arena has been a source of surprise to those who comment on our world today. One of them has suggested that the 1990s could well become known as the decade of religious nationalism.[5] The image of supposedly religious groups of people fighting each other with great passion and violence is one that is often seen in the media these days, making it more urgent than ever that the world's religions can be seen as able to live at peace together.

REASSESSMENT

The third way of responding to these changes in society, I want to call 'reassessment'. This involves, like the previous group, making decisions about what is essential to a particular religious tradition and what is not, but in a more open and flexible, perhaps a more risky, way. Evangelical Christians may, for example, decide that the Bible still has to be the foundational document for the faith but that it can be studied in a critical way, and that the Holy Spirit can lead Christians to new ways of interpreting and understanding it. Some Muslims have responded to the changing world by going back to the Qur'an in a similarly deferential but searching way. Catholic Christians may decide that the Church still has the authority to interpret the Bible and the movement of the Spirit for them, but, as happened quite dramatically during Vatican II in the 1960s, this does not mean that the Church can't be open to change or move forward with the times. Some Orthodox Jews may similarly believe that while the traditional interpretation of the Torah by the rabbis of old must still be observed, modern problems require modern solutions and there is continuing work to be done.

Part of this reassessment will include people facing the fact of plurality—that their religion, and the particular way they interpret and practise it, is one among many; that sincere, pious and good-living people believe quite different things from them about the way the world is and about the spiritual reality that lies behind it. It will, however, also involve not abandoning their religious roots, their scriptures, institutions or traditions, but returning to them with a different viewpoint, to work at them again, towards finding a new understanding of how to use and apply them in a different world.

ASSIMILATION

The last way of responding is to take this process even further and allow one's religious community to become assimilated into the surrounding culture. Scripture and past traditions may no longer be seen as having any authority, but regarded as useful background material, while one's own thinking and feeling develops, guided by the ideas and values that guide the rest of the society. Supernatural stories and explanations will be treated as outdated myths and the modern values of tolerance, justice, open-mindedness and inclusiveness will prevail to form a new ethic. Old rituals and symbols may be abandoned or reinterpreted and new forms of worship devised. These movements, like the Quakers perhaps, liberal Judaism and Christianity, or some parts of the charismatic movement, can be popular options for the emerging generation and may keep younger members of the more conservative groups from drifting away from their religion altogether.

These different ways that religious people have responded to the arrival of so many social changes can be seen to be different answers to the questions 'How far can we go?' and 'How far must we go?' in moving our theology and practice on, so that our beliefs and way of life can remain relevant and viable and yet keep a sufficiently firm hold on its roots and traditions to survive.

CHAPTER 4

SEEING CHRISTIANITY
AS ONE FAITH AMONG MANY

I heard someone say on a television discussion recently, 'I don't want to see Christianity as one religion among many.' I can appreciate how he felt, but in England in the 21st century this seems to me a bit like the ostriches who, when they feel threatened, put their heads in the sand. Christianity *is* one religion among many in Britain today and, for many of us, in our local communities. However much people want to argue that their particular kind of Christianity is different, or that other faiths don't count as proper religions, it is a fact that people around us make just the same sort of claims for their beliefs. In view of the variety of beliefs to be found within our own faith worldwide, it could almost be true to say that there are several different religions within Christianity, so our own version of Christianity is one among many interpretations of the significance of the life, death and resurrection of Jesus. Conceding these facts does not have immediate implications for the truth of our own or anyone else's beliefs, although it does rather change the way we look at the world.

Studying religions from what you might call an 'outsider perspective' is a quite recent activity in the academic world, and one that may seem strange to people deeply involved in a religion themselves. Students starting on courses run by a Religious Studies department will be told that they need to become detached observers—to suspend, for the time being, ideas about truth and value and to ask critical questions not only about other people's worldviews, but also about their own, whether these be secular or religious. Some people find this easier than others, but I think that everyone finds it, at times, both unnerving and quite exciting.

People travelling in order to spread their own faith in foreign cultures often make a deliberate effort to look at the faiths of the people they hope to meet, in as objective a way as possible. Now, however, as the world shrinks, anyone who takes their faith seriously and wants to engage with people outside their own faith community will find that they need to be able to stand back in this way.

I often begin the course I teach by asking the students to think up a definition of a religion, and to think not only in terms of what religions are, but also what they are for. Dictionaries can be some help but, especially in the older ones, you can sometimes detect a rather Western bias. Words can be perfectly useful, even in an academic context, without having tight definitions. We usually consider several ways of looking at the human phenomenon of religious belief and then I leave it open for the students to develop their idea of what religions are and what they do for people and societies, as the course proceeds.

WHAT IS A RELIGION?

Here is one definition that I find quite a helpful starting point: 'a religion is a set of stories, beliefs and activities (some people like the word 'rituals') that a community uses to construct and express its sense of identity and values'. You might never have thought of Christianity quite like that, but I'm sure you can see that, as one of many religions in the world, it does fit into this description rather well.

Students who are 'on the ball' will quickly see that many things not usually thought of as genuine religions fit this description too— secular ideologies like Marxism or humanism, science, or even football, can function in this way for certain groups of people. Some students decide that they don't want these ideas and activities to be included in their definition of religion. They must be careful, though, about suggesting the inclusion of 'belief in God', in the sense of a personal, omnipotent being, since this will exclude some forms of Eastern religions that most people definitely do want to be included in their definitions. So they might add something about the presence of 'ideas that transcend the material world'.

There have, of course, been thousands of different religions in the history of the world, many of which are still practised today. For the purposes of this book, however, we will be confining our study to the umbrella of six great world religious systems under which the vast majority of religious communities in the world today find a shelter—Judaism, Christianity and Islam, Hinduism, Buddhism and Sikhism.

WHERE DO RELIGIONS START?

A good way to start thinking about religions as a whole is to try to find where they start, not historically but ideologically—the situation or predicament for which they claim to have answers. It does seem to be the case that all religions start with a universally recurring feeling about the unsatisfactoriness of human life. It's not that, as Thomas Hobbes put it rather dramatically, all human lives are lived 'in continual fear and danger of violent death', or that the 'life of man [is] solitary, poor, nasty, brutish and short',[6] although this has undoubtedly been true of many lives at every point of human history. The rock star and humanitarian campaigner Bob Geldof KMG expresses the feeling of dissatisfaction in a way that we might identify with more closely, when he poses the question in the title of his autobiography, 'Is That It?'[7] People who live in prosperous, complacent societies probably feel it least, but most of us who reflect on the nature of human life feel something of this mismatch between our expectations and hopes—how we feel life ought to be and how it actually is. For while human life seems to have enormous potential for goodness, creativity and joy, this

potential is so rarely achieved or maintained, and is always spoilt—
if by nothing else, by the spectre of death. Writers like Thomas
Hardy (1840–1928) and Jean Paul Sartre (1905–80) open up this
feeling for us in their novels, but are thin on ways of resolving it.

Religions can be seen to attempt to explain what has gone wrong
with life and to give people goals to aim for and programmes to help
reach those goals. What I find most interesting is that, looking at
the six main world religions as a whole, although there are con-
spicuous differences in the stories they tell and in the beliefs they
hold, one can pick out a great deal that is shared in the explanation
of the problems of being human, and in the answers offered—ways
of seeing what life ought to be like and how we could move towards
the goal of reaching our potential as human beings.

Let's look at some of these explanations and answers. Religious
thought, across the world, characteristically explains the unsatisfactoriness of human life in terms of ignorance, powerlessness and
alienation. As human beings, we are born in a very helpless state, not
knowing much that we seem to need or want to know about the
material world around us and how it works, and about how to
organize and control our social world, or even the private world of
our thinking and feeling. We don't know if our lives and relationships
have any wider meaning, significance or destiny beyond what we see
here, although most human communities, ever since there have been
such things, have had the underlying feeling (or wish, perhaps) that
it must be so. This awareness of ignorance leads to a sense of
powerlessness. There is so much that we feel we can't control in our
natural world, in our social life and in our own personalities. These
feelings can be experienced as a sort of alienation—being cut off
from the source of goodness and life, truth and power, out of touch
with one another and with our deeper selves.

Building cultures is the way human beings cope with this
situation—cultures that in the modern world are fragmented into
different spheres like science, education, politics, history, art and
religion. This gives us the feeling that we can make sense of, and
be safe and confident in, a largely mysterious world. Nuala Ni

Dhomhnaill, in a poem I particularly like, talks of having to 'make do with today's happenings and stoop and somehow glue together the silly little shards of our lives, so that our children can drink water from broken bowls, not from cupped hands.'[8]

The sciences give us knowledge about the natural world and how it works; sociology and politics find facts to help us understand and control our social life; psychology and ethics try to help us understand ourselves; the arts give us insights into life at every level; but still there are deeper questions about who we are and what we could be. These are the questions that religions can be seen to tackle.

WHAT GOALS DO THEY SET?

In the world religions, ignorance is often explained as a sort of blindness, or illusion: our perception is clouded in some way, so that we are not seeing things as they really are. So they offer a way towards enlightenment, a different sort of perception, as a way to find the truth. They might also connect our feeling of ignorance with the idea of being alienated, or cut off from the spiritual reality that lies behind our material existence. So the answer is to find a source of truth about that reality. All the six main world religions that we will be looking at in this book include, within their many forms, the idea of revelation—of wisdom and knowledge coming from the spiritual realm as well as being the product of human deliberation and creativity.

To combat feelings of powerlessness, the main world religions offer us liberation and empowerment, the chance to be freed from all that traps, entangles and blinds us, a way to find the power to live life more authentically. They promise ways of overcoming feelings of alienation—of finding union or communion with, becoming part of or achieving a relationship with, the divine; finding a community that works; or getting in touch with our real selves.

WHAT WAYS ARE THERE OF REACHING THESE GOALS?

If the predicament of human beings is seen as a problem with ignorance, powerlessness and alienation, and the goals of a religious life as finding truth, liberation and union, what ways do the main religions propose to overcome this predicament and reach these goals? I would like to divide them into four—the way of ritual, the way of law, the way of grace and the way of mysticism. The interesting thing about the six main world religions is that they are all practised in so many different forms around the world that all these ways can be found within all of them. As we look more closely at each way, I expect you will be able to see that they are all present in Christianity, and have been emphasized in different ways by different groups, at different times and in different places.

A ritual can be defined as a repeated action or activity that has a symbolic meaning for a particular community. Within all the religions we are looking at, there are groups of people who can see that rituals, in this sense, can be corrupted into meaningless activities, but the word can cover even the most informal gatherings or private activities. I want to include under this heading all worship and prayer, festivals and celebrations—those sorts of symbolic actions that make past events present and real for their participants. I want to include singing and dancing, making offerings and sacrifices, all praising, contemplating, propitiating or invoking the divine, all requests for protection, forgiveness, blessing and guidance. Rituals, in this sense, give people's lives shape, meaning and direction, create a sense of community and affirm a sense of values; they are a way of making contact with the divine, and so of achieving all those goals we have been thinking about.

The way of law is the pursuit of righteousness—the discovery of how to live well. Often this is seen in terms of submission to the divine will, obedience to revealed rules or principles or the discovery of a natural moral order within or behind the material universe and an attempt to live in harmony with it. The importance of morality, of living right, is present in all the main world religions and to some it has a prominent place in achieving those religious goals.

The way of grace is the discovery that there is a supernatural source of unmerited favour that can be received through faith and devotion. It is about finding mercy and reconciliation—all that is implied in the idea of salvation as a gift. Again, it is an idea that emerges in some form in all of the six main world religions and is strongly emphasized by some groups in most of them.

The way of mysticism or, to use a more contemporary but also more nebulous word, of spirituality, is the way of opening up new sorts of perception—seeing things differently (some would say, seeing things as they really are). It can involve achieving altered states of consciousness so that the world of the spirit can be experienced and, in some cases, take control. This can be done through prayer, music, physical movement, through the techniques of meditation and through asceticism. It finds expression in significant movements in Judaism and Islam. Always there in the background of Christianity, this way of overcoming those feelings of ignorance, powerlessness and alienation has recently reemerged in the Pentecostal and charismatic movements. It pervades all the Eastern religions.

In this chapter, we have looked very briefly at Christianity as one religion among many, which may have been a new experience for some readers. We have been looking from an outside perspective at religions as an aspect of human culture, suspending for the time being judgments about the truth and value of this whole way of looking at human life, as well as the different explanations and answers that the religions offer.

It is important that people in today's world are able to do this, to acknowledge and understand to some extent that not everyone sees the world in the same way as they do. Religions and other aspects of human cultures, such as language, literature, history and art, are what provide people's worldview. They are the glasses through which we see the world, giving us the ideas and the words we need to interpret our experiences. They instruct us in what truth and value mean and how to find them. Not acknowledging this can so easily lead to misunderstanding, to isolation, fear and conflict. We need to listen to each other, so that we can start to see how the world looks from where other people stand, and invite them to 'come and see how the world looks from here'.

LISTENING TO PEOPLE
OF OTHER FAITHS

INTRODUCTION

Towards the end of October 2002, I set about collecting material for this book. I decided to limit my research to the six main world faiths—Judaism, Christianity and Islam, Hinduism, Buddhism and Sikhism. Following up all the contacts and leads I had—friends, colleagues, students, neighbours, local interfaith groups and occasionally the telephone directory—I visited eight different communities and places of worship and spoke to ten people in their homes or places of work.

It's important to say from the start that there is no way this selection of people is representative of these faith communities in London, let alone in the world. Just as I could have interviewed hundreds of Christians—Baptists, Coptics, Methodists and Mennonites, Anglo-Catholics and fundamentalists—and got hundreds of different answers, but chose just three, so the people from these faith communities speak only for themselves. The aim of these conversations is not to inform you of the beliefs and practices of these religions, but to enable you to listen to the people whose lives they shape.

Some of the people I spoke to are eminent leaders and teachers, like the Mufti from our local mosque, the International Coordinator of Women from the Swaminarayan Movement and the rabbi from the Masorti Synagogue. I spoke to a Hindu monk and a Christian friar and a senior member of the Western Buddhist Order. Others are just ordinary followers, at different stages in their religious journeys. Most are still in the religion of their birth but some are converts to a new religion. What they all have in common is that their faith is important to them. It should probably be borne in mind that I contacted some of these people through various interfaith networks, as they most strongly supported the project and were the most eager to take part, but there are plenty of others here too, to give a fairly balanced view.

Although the aim was that these conversations would be open and relaxed, I did have a set of questions that most people saw before we met, to give them an idea of the sort of issues I wanted to explore. I've listed them below so that you know, in very broad terms, how the conversations were structured.

- Do you belong to a religious community or tradition, or are you committed to a particular religious way of life? Can you tell me a little about it?
- Do you have a special role in it?
- When and how did you come to be committed in this way?
- In what ways do you think your religious commitment helps you to live a better life (in any sense of that word 'better')?
- What are the general problems or difficulties about human life that your faith addresses?
- What answers or ways of resolving or coping with these problems does it offer you?
- What would you say was the ultimate goal of your religious life and activity?
- How does your religion help you reach that goal?
- How confident are you that you will reach it?
- How do you know about the spiritual reality that you believe lies behind human existence, and what the implications of this are to how you ought to live?
- Do you feel that in any sense you make contact with, or get to know, this reality?
- What part, if any, do prayer, worship, meditation or ritual play in your religious life and what do you gain from them?
- How certain are you that your religious tradition represents the truth and how important do you think it is that other people should believe it too?

I added at the bottom, 'Please don't feel limited or constrained by these questions, but free to say, in any way you would like to put it, what your faith means to you.'

The next chapter contains some background information about the six religions followed by the people I interviewed. You can either read this through now or use it to dip into as you come to different sections of the conversations. The aim is that it will help you to listen with a little more understanding.

CHAPTER FIVE

SIX WORLD RELIGIONS

When we listen to friends and colleagues, even people quite close to us, we are sometimes puzzled by what they say, not because we don't understand the words, but because we can't imagine what experiences and thoughts could have raised those questions in their minds or led them to hold such opinions. In this situation, information about what has been happening in their lives, who they have been talking to or what they have been reading can often help us.

When a colleague of mine, who was an Anglican clergyman, announced one day that he was leaving the Church of England, resigning from his job, although he had no immediate plans for how he would earn a living or keep his family, we were puzzled. Was his congregation that difficult? Were his family that unhappy? Had his sense of vocation crumbled? Then he gave us something to read about the Puritans, their ideas about the importance of personal conscience and how it had inspired them in their stormy relationship with the established Church in the 17th century. With that piece of information, what he was saying began to make sense.

Listening to people who look at the world from a very different vantage-point from ours can be even more puzzling, and any information we can collect about their lives, their faith, their culture, their worldview, will help us to listen with more understanding. It is not the purpose of this book to open up the scriptures, philosophy, history, beliefs and practices of the world's religions. It is too vast a subject. We shall be listening to people from just six religions, so here are some simple notes to provide a very basic outline of how these religions started, how they are related and divided, and to give a sense of the enormous variety of beliefs and practices found within each of them.

WHY THESE SIX RELIGIONS?

Way back in the early history of the human race, each little tribal community would have had its own rituals to perform and stories to tell, to express its own beliefs about the meaning and destiny of life, who they were and what they feared and valued. As the population of the world grew and moved around, and these people-groups lived in closer communication with one another, their stories and beliefs merged and mingled, developed and trans-formed, died out, split and spread. Groups often defined by geo-graphy, class or gender took these powerful materials, moulded, promoted and used them to enlighten, liberate and empower, to inspire and encourage, to define and exclude, to control, exploit and oppress. Later in history, secular ideologies like Marxism and humanism, with their stories and rituals, took their place too. Over the centuries, the world scene came to be dominated by the worldviews that had proved most durable in some sense. Were they perhaps those stories and rituals that were the most useful, the most powerful, the most flexible, the most enthusiastically or effectively promoted?

So what is the scene today? It is notoriously difficult to put together reliable statistics on the numbers of people who align themselves with different belief systems or use different religious practices, but from available sources[8] it is possible to calculate that towards the end of the 20th century there were around nine hundred million people in the world who could be classed as either atheist or having a non-religious worldview. Over three thousand million followed what are often called the Semitic religions, Judaism and the religions that grew out of it—Christianity and Islam. Around one thousand million practised what are often called the Indian religions, Hinduism and the religions that grew out of that—

including Buddhism and Sikhism. Another nearly four hundred million people were credited with following other religions, including the ancient Chinese religions of Daoism and Confucianism and tribal religions of one sort or another.

According to these figures, then, roughly three quarters of the world's population today are in some way connected with six major religions. We can divide these six into two groups, one that began in the Middle East with the Semitic races (Abraham's descendants) and has since travelled mainly west, and the other that began in India and has travelled mainly east. The remaining quarter of the world's population are roughly divided between what we might call minority religions and those who follow no religion at all.

It is hard to imagine how these figures were collected, or what criteria were used for putting people in one category rather than another. Each of these religions is practised in a wide variety of ways, and at different levels of commitment, and each contains around its periphery many people and groups whose right to be considered as genuine members of the religion is disputed by others within it. You need only to think who among your acquaintances you would count as being Christian, atheist or Muslim and how this could relate to any official statistics that are available, to see the problem. The figures do, however, give us some indication of the influence of these six religions in the world today.

TWO ANCIENT RELIGIONS

The three Semitic religions we are looking at have grown from the root of ancient Judaism. The three Indian religions have grown from the root of ancient Hinduism. These two ancient religions have some interesting similarities and some very significant differences that flavour the religions that developed from them.

Both start with old writings—some of the most ancient literature in the world. These writings tell of migration, of ritual sacrifice, of revelation of eternal truths from another sphere. Both develop moral laws that lay down rules about the preservation and organization of their societies. Both move on to include ideas about the need for people to be freed from self-centredness by becoming aware of a spiritual dimension to their lives.

One of the biggest differences between the religions of the East and of the West is their view of the histories of the material world and of the individual, for according to the Semitic worldview these histories are finite and linear; they have a beginning and they have an end. We hear the ongoing story of creation, fall, redemption and then recreation; and, for the individual, birth, the discovery of God, death and then what lies beyond. According to the Eastern worldview, however, there is an eternal, cyclical view of these histories, with the continual recreation of ages and worlds and the continual reincarnation of souls, until they can break free.

The Western religions tend to see the divine as one unique spiritual being, in many ways separate from the material universe that he has created. Worshippers are warned of the dangers of using material things as images or representations of God. Christianity in some ways breaks this pattern when it tells of God entering the world in Jesus and, in the thinking of many Christians, in the symbols of bread and wine in Holy Communion.

Eastern Orthodoxy has a more Eastern view of the relationship between the material and the spiritual. In the Indian religions, God, who is often described as the Supreme Being or as Ultimate Reality, is usually seen to be more immanent in the material world—even to the extent of the material world being, in some senses, his body. God therefore can be manifested, become accessible, to people in all sorts of material things, animate and inanimate—trees, rivers and animals, images and Gurus. The Buddha, while denying the existence of a supreme creator, taught of a multiplicity of heavenly beings; and Guru Nanak, the founder of the Sikh religion, in some ways breaks this mould too when he teaches in his hymns that all the images and rituals of Hinduism can't compare with hearing, obeying and loving God in your heart.

SALVATION

In both worldviews human life is seen as inherently unsatisfactory, there being a better, happier, more authentic way of being human that is attainable through religious ideas and practices. This idea is often described as 'salvation'. Salvation in the Semitic religions is typically seen as being saved from the consequences of rebellion against or disobedience to the Creator, which alienates people from him. The goal is to be reconnected, to find harmony, peace or union with God through righteousness, by living a godly or God-centred life and by finding his forgiveness. In the Indian religions, salvation is typically seen as being saved from ignorance, from an illusion that traps us in a self-centred material world. The goal is to be liberated from this trap by reaching a new sort of perception, seeing the truth, and this is achieved by a number of equally valid ways including right living, learning to control the mind, and devotion to a gracious Lord.

These are the broadest brush strokes imaginable: you can find exceptions everywhere and they can't start to cover the variety of ideas and practices that have mingled and cross-fertilized to produce the multitude of beliefs that we see around us in today's world.

In the notes that follow, I have included what I think are the most significant people, books and events in the development of our six religions with some very short comments about each of them. The choice of what to include and what to say about them is necessarily arbitrary and somewhat controversial. Many of the dates given for people's births or for events (especially the ones marked with a 'c') are very approximate and sometimes quite vigorously disputed, both by academics and by people within the religions. The dates of the various writings are particularly vague and in some cases just mark the end of a very long process.

It is usual, when including other religions than Christianity in a historical discussion, to use the letters CE, referring to the Common Era, rather than AD (from the Latin phrase *Anno Domini*, 'in the year of our Lord'), and the letters BCE (Before the Common Era) rather than BC (Before Christ), and I have followed this precedent. The other religions have their own dating systems, based on the most significant dates in their histories, but usually conform to this system too when they are including a discussion of other religions.

PEOPLE FROM THE SEMITIC RELIGIONS

(The dates in this section are of people's births, as far as they are known.)

BCE

c.2000 Abraham: According to the biblical story, Abraham came originally from Ur (possibly in Iraq). He was called by God to set out to a new country and was promised that he would father a race that would inherit its own land and through whom God would bring about the redemption of the world.

c.1250 Moses: After the tribe of Abraham had been enslaved in Egypt, Moses led them to freedom. During the journey to their 'promised land', later called Israel, it is believed that God made a covenant with the people that included revealing detailed laws and rituals to them through Moses.

c.6 Jesus Christ: 'Christ' is the Greek version of the title 'Messiah' given to Jesus of Nazareth by his Jewish followers, who saw him as the long-promised redeemer. Crucified by the Romans, his death is believed to have been a divine self-sacrifice for the sins of the world, vindicated by his rising from the dead. Jesus lives on in his Church by the Holy Spirit.

CE

274 Constantine: This Roman emperor, after years of persecuting Christians, declared Christianity a tolerated religion, leading to its being adopted as the official religion of the Roman empire.

570 Muhammad: Through a series of visions Muhammad dictated the contents of the Qur'an, which was accepted by his followers as a direct and final revelation from Allah, the God of Abraham and Jesus. He set up a body of followers, the Muslim community, which rapidly spread through the Arab world and beyond.

1134 Maimonides: A medieval Jewish theologian who codified all the Jewish laws and rituals. He outlined what he thought were the essential dogmas of the Jewish faith.

1483 Martin Luther: A Christian monk who is credited with having provoked the Protestant Reformation in Germany by his insistence that justification is by grace, through faith alone, and that the authority of the Bible is supreme over church tradition.

1703 John Wesley: One of the prime movers in a far-reaching revival that began in England, founding at the same time Methodism and English Evangelicalism.

PEOPLE FROM THE INDIAN RELIGIONS

BCE

c.480 Gautama Buddha: Buddha, meaning 'enlightened one', is a title given to Gautama, a Hindu prince who, through meditation, reached a state of enlightenment about the nature of human existence, which is believed to result in release from rebirth. He set up communities of monks and nuns to explore and spread his teaching.

273 Ashoka: An emperor of India who embraced Buddhism and thus established it as the national religion. He sent out missionaries to other lands where the religion was enthusiastically received, but by 1200CE Buddhism had almost completely disappeared from India.

CE

788 Sankara: A Hindu priest and philosopher who harmonized the teaching of the Upanishads into a coherent system, with a single Divine Reality that permeates the whole universe and is identical with the soul of the individual. Knowledge of this Reality can be achieved through meditation, but it can, at a lower level, be worshipped as a personal Lord.

1017 Ramanuja: A Hindu philosopher who expressed an interpretation of the Upanishads more tuned towards a personal creator God and the need for God's grace in the quest for salvation.

1133 Honen: A Japanese teacher of Buddhism who introduced the Pure Land sect (begun in China around 400CE) into Japan. He rejected monasticism and other traditional Buddhist practices, saying that divine initiative must take the place of human effort. He pointed his followers to scriptures that tell of another Buddha (Amida) vowing to save those who call on his name and give them rebirth in his 'Pure Land'. Now one of the largest Buddhist sects in Japan.

1469 Guru Nanak: The first of the ten Sikh Gurus (or spiritual teachers) and the founder of the Sikh religion, originally a sect of Hinduism but quite quickly accepted as a separate religion. His teaching denounced many contemporary Hindu practices and taught of one God who reveals himself and with whom anyone can have a direct inner relationship through God's generosity, without the trappings of external religious practices.

1666 Guru Gobind Singh: The last of the ten Sikh Gurus, who instituted the Khalsa order. By taking on the distinctive symbols of Sikhism, most notably today in the wearing of a turban, both men and women can adopt a militant and visible identity. He declared that the Sikh's holy book was their Guru and did not appoint a successor, saying that they would now be led by the book and the community.

1863 Vivekananda: An important figure in modern Hinduism. He travelled around India and North America spreading the teaching of the saintly mystic Ramakrishna (1834). He established the Ramakrishna mission, which makes the relief of human suffering its main duty.

1869 Mahatma Gandhi: Mahatma (Reverend) is a title ascribed to Mohandas Gandhi, a Hindu reformer who, inspired by the Bhagavad Gita, taught a way of selfless action and non-violence.

BOOKS FROM THE SEMITIC RELIGIONS

(These dates are particularly vague and often just mark the end of a very long process.)

BCE

c.1250–500 Torah: The Torah, literally 'teaching', is a term widely used in Judaism, but in a narrow sense it refers to the first five books of the Bible. Orthodox Jews believe that it was given to Moses by God in a direct revelation as part of his covenant with the Jewish people. Alongside it is an oral Torah passed down from Moses by word of mouth and eventually written down as the Mishnah. Most Christians accept the original written Torah as part of 'the word of God' but believe that Jesus has superseded most of the detailed regulations it contains.

c.400 Writings and Prophets/Old Testament: The rest of the Jewish Bible and Christian Old Testament, this collection contains songs, poems, history, wisdom literature and the writings of the prophets. It is extensively used in Jewish and Christian worship.

CE

c.50–90 New Testament: This covers the rest of the Christian scriptures and includes the four Gospels—the life and teaching of Jesus seen by four different writers, traditionally held to have been eyewitnesses or to have got their material from eyewitnesses. The

New Testament also includes letters written by early church leaders, mostly by Paul. Most Christians treat the whole Bible as inspired and authoritative.

c.500 Talmud: The writings of the Jewish Rabbis and the main source of Jewish law, containing the Mishnah and extensive commentaries on it and on the Torah. It is considered legally binding on all orthodox Jews.

650 Qur'an: The sacred book of the Muslims, who believe it is an eternal text, revealed to Muhammad over a period of a few years and successively dictated to followers who eventually wrote it down. The text, in the original Arabic, is sacred in itself and the book and its contents are treated with great reverence and used for liturgical and devotional purposes as well being as the basis of Muslim law.

c.900 Hadith: Several collections of traditional stories about Muhammad and other prominent early Muslims, that are also used to interpret and apply the Qur'an in the development of Muslim law.

BOOKS FROM THE INDIAN RELIGIONS

BCE

c.1400–1200 Rig Veda: Complied by the Aryans who probably migrated into India from the north-west, this is the first part of a body of works collectively known as Veda, which means 'sacred knowledge'. The Veda, as a whole collection, is accepted as eternal truth, revealed and authoritative, by most Hindus. They use the term *shruti* for it, which means 'what is heard'. Rig Veda is a collection of hymns and instructions for ancient sacrifices.

c.400 Upanishads: A later addition to the Veda, these writings are more theological and philosophical. Most scholarly Hindu thought since c.400 is based largely on the exegesis and interpretation of these writings.

c.300 Pali Canon: The accepted scriptures of Buddhism (which are written in the language of Pali). These are believed to be the sayings and discourses of the Buddha, orally preserved by his disciples, who met shortly after his death to recite, agree and authenticate them, although they were not written down until many years later. The Buddha taught that his words were not sacrosanct and should not be taken on trust but investigated and tested. There are many commentaries, notably Buddhaghosa's *Path to Purity*, which was written in the 5th century and established Theraveda orthodoxy. In the other main stream of the religion, Mahayana Buddhists use the Pali Canon to different extents, plus a large number of Sutras, some of which are believed to have been revealed by Gautama Buddha after his death or by other supernatural beings.

c.300BCE–100CE Bhagavad Gita: This is a short section from the Mahabharata, one of the longest epic poems in the world. It tells of the intervention in a civil war of Krishna, an avatar, or incarnation, of Vishnu, the Supreme God. It draws together many different elements in Hindu thought with the message that there are several different ways to salvation. Although not given the status of revealed scripture, it is probably the most popular book for modern Hindus.

c.200BCE–200CE Manusmriti: The earliest of the Hindu law books, which set out the moral and ritual duties of the different genders, classes and stages of life.

CE1500–1708 Guru Granth Sahib: The holy book of the Sikh religion, this contains the hymns of Guru Nanak and some of the other Gurus and other religious poets, both Hindu and Muslim. It is revered as if it were a living Guru and is the focus of attention in all Sikh rituals and festivals and the content of their daily worship, leading to Sikhism being called a 'religion of the book'.

EVENTS FROM THE SEMITIC RELIGIONS

(Dates are again often rather arbitrary, marking in several cases some significant feature of a long process.)

BCE

c.1250 Exodus from Egypt: The Bible tells the story of how the Israelite tribes were freed from slavery in Egypt and set off for their promised land under the leadership of Moses—an event that is commemorated annually as the Passover.

587 Exile to Babylon: The Babylonians captured Jerusalem, destroying the temple and carrying its inhabitants off as exiles. The Jews returned about 50 years later, when Babylon was defeated by Persia and rebuilt the city and its temple under Zerubbabel.

CE

70 Diaspora: After an uprising against the Romans, the city of Jerusalem was taken, its temple finally destroyed and its people dispersed into the surrounding nations.

680 Massacre at Karbala: A disagreement about the leadership of the Muslim community led to Ali, Muhammad's cousin and son-in-law, being killed. Of his two sons, considered by a group known as Shi'ah to be rightful leaders, Hasan was murdered, and when Hussain challenged the leadership he and his followers were wiped out in a massacre—an event that is commemorated annually by Shi'ah Muslims. They see in the death of Hussain vicarious redemption through his suffering. Sunni Muslims are now the majority, with most Shi'ah Muslims living in Iran, where it is the official religion of the state.

1054 The Great Schism: Communion was broken off between the Christian East (Orthodox) and the Christian West (Catholic) after a long conflict over diverse issues of theology and practice, politics and power. The Eastern Orthodox became a federation of self-governing, often national, churches, the Catholic West a single powerful institution led by its popes.

1453 Conquest of Constantinople by the Ottoman Empire: After driving the Eastern Christian (Byzantine) empire out of what is modern Turkey, the militant Muslim Ottoman empire conquered the symbolic, part-European city of Constantinople. Their dominance over vast areas of Asia, Europe and Africa did not begin to decline until around 1600 and collapsed after the First World War.

1517 Protestant Reformation: A movement for reform from within the Catholic Church, which asserted the authority of the Bible over that of the Church and of salvation by grace, through faith, rather than through human effort or the sacraments of the Church. This led to a permanent split in Western Christianity, spawning numerous Protestant denominations.

1800 Jewish Reform Movement: A movement to update Judaism in response to Enlightenment ideas began in Germany and spread to America. It revised the liturgy and absorbed new critical methods of historical and literary research to question the origins and use of Judaism's ancient literature. Liberal Judaism followed later and went further. Their followers are together referred to as Progressive Jews.

1800 The age of Christian missionary expansion: While the Roman Catholic Church had been taking the gospel to Asia, the Americas and beyond since its own Counter-Reformation in the 16th century, Protestant missionary work took off later, sparked by the 18th-century Evangelical revival and the rise of British trade and colonialism. It was during this period that Christianity became a world religion.

1917 Jews return to Israel: After the breakdown of the Ottoman empire, British rule in Palestine allowed Jews to return with the hope of setting up their own state, a dream of the Zionist movement active since 1897. When the British left, war between Jews and Arabs led, in 1948, to a ceasefire and uneasy partition agreement.

1933–45 Holocaust: Six million Jews died in central and eastern Europe in the Nazi extermination programme.

1947 The founding of Pakistan: The end of British rule in India involved the setting up of one of the first modern Islamic states, the eastern part of which split off in 1972 to form the separate state of Bangladesh.

1965 The Second Vatican Council Reports: The Roman Catholic Church responded to the modern world by making some remarkable changes in attitudes and practices, many of which have since been muted by a conservative Pope.

1979 Revolution in Iran: In a popular, violent uprising the Shah was deposed and the exiled religious leader Ayatollah Khomeini returned to establish a government. After a 98 per cent 'Yes' vote, Iran was declared an Islamic state, marking a resurgence of confidence in the world's Muslim community.

EVENTS FROM THE INDIAN RELIGIONS

BCE

c.1500 Migration of Aryans: Whether this was an invasion or a gradual migration (or whether it happened at all) is disputed, but the early Hindu scripture, the Veda, is deemed to be the work of a people calling themselves Arya (or noble) who flourished in northwest India, with their own language and priestly religion of sacrifices, hymns and social organization. As they spread down through India, the Aryan culture mingled with the religion and culture of the existing population.

c.300 Second Buddhist Council: The Buddha's followers met for a second time about 100 years after his death. It was around this time that disagreements began to lead to a split within Buddhism, which grew gradually and peacefully into two branches—the Theravada (now practised mainly in Sri Lanka and southern Asia) which claims to keep closer to the original teaching of the Buddha, and the Mahayana (found in eastern and northern Asia, including China, Japan and Tibet), which emerged as an enormously diverse development of the original teaching in different cultural contexts, based on a wide variety of different texts, practices and experiences.

c.100 Buddhism in China: The Buddha's followers travelled the trade routes of the East and took their religion with them. Indian culture in general and Buddhism in particular were enthusiastically received and merged with Taoism and other Chinese ideas and practices to produce a variety of new forms. Emperor Huan is recorded on a memorial set up in 166CE as worshipping at Buddhist shrines. Buddhism was suppressed during Communist rule.

c.400 Pure Land Buddhism: In this new form of Chinese Buddhism, Amitabha, a Buddha from a previous age, is believed to have vowed to enable those devoted to him to be reborn in his Pure Land, where they will attain enlightenment. Devotees chant his name, worship his image and sing hymns to him.

c.600 Buddhism in Japan: Buddhism arrived in Japan from Korea around 550. After some opposition from the Shinto priests, it was well received. Under Shotoku, Prince Regent from 594CE, it became part of the state apparatus, where it coexisted happily with other indigenous religions until 1860, when Shinto was declared Japan's official religion.

c.750 Buddhism in Tibet: Buddhism arrived gradually in Tibet and took on several unique and contrasting forms. Since the Chinese invasion in 1950 it has been suppressed, but Tibetan Buddhism is one of the forms that has taken root in the West.

1947 End of British rule in India: In spite of Gandhi's efforts to keep peace, this led to violent conflict between Hindus, Muslims and Sikhs as borders were set up and people were forced to migrate.

1959 The Dalai Lama escapes from Tibet: The religious and political leader of Tibet, believed by his followers to be an incarnation of a Bodhisattva (a Buddhist supernatural being), fled from the Chinese invading force and became an international religious figure.

1984 Assault on the Golden Temple: The Indian Prime Minister, Indira Gandhi, ordered the Indian army to attack Amritsar, the sacred centre of Sikhism, to flush out a violent Sikh reformer who had taken shelter there. Sikhs all over the world responded with anger at the sacrilege, damage and loss of life, and many returned to the distinctive symbols of their religion. Indira Gandhi was assassinated later in the same year by her Sikh bodyguards, causing more violent reactions.

1998 Hindu National Party comes to power in India: The BJP, an ultra-nationalist political party which defines India and its culture as Hindu, came to power, raising anxiety for minority religions.

Think of that famous photograph of our planet, taken in the 1960s from space. This is the world that God loves, that Christians believe Jesus died to save—this globalized, pluralistic and still incorrigibly religious world. We're going to listen now to some of the inhabitants of this world as they talk about their faith.

As you read these conversations, try to imagine you are sitting in the rabbi's living-room with the dog snoring at his feet, or in the colourful vegetarian café at the Tibetan Buddhist centre with clatter and chatter all around—meeting people very like yourself, talking openly and honestly about how their religion works for them in their daily lives.

It's not easy, but try to listen, in the first place, with as open a mind as you can, not making evaluations or comparisons, not wanting to see everything from your own point of view, nor dismissing things that you can't understand or that seem to challenge your own beliefs. Try just to listen.

CHAPTER 6

LISTENING TO HINDUS

The Hindu community in London is justly proud of the fabulous white marble temple they have built in Neasden and this was my first point of contact with them. Turning off the North Circular Road opposite the sprawling concrete and steel edifice that is the IKEA furniture store, it is a stunningly incongruous and startling experience to come across the temple, especially at night.

I had arranged to meet Nitin Palan, the temple's voluntary interfaith representative, and he organized a tour of the temple complex for me, with its efficiently staffed reception area complete with shop and shoe racks, a vegetarian kitchen, an ornately decorated and strangely peaceful shrine room, and enormous prayer hall, that can seat three thousand people. The complex is open for anyone all day and buzzed with worshippers and visitors.

Nitin Palan took me to see the image of 'his Lord', Swami Nayaran (1781–1830), who founded this movement within Hinduism around 1800 and whom they speak of as an incarnation of God. He has been followed by a succession of Swamis or divine leaders, the present one being Pramukh Swami Maharaj (b. 1921).

NITIN PALAN

Nitin told me:

'We call the creator the Supreme Lord. Some people call it Father, some people call it God. This creator is someone who comes to life: [then] some people call it Prophet, some people call it Son. It's just different terminology, different statements. This creator, who comes to us in different forms and different shapes and different places and different names, gives everybody experiences, whether Christian, Muslim, Jain, Sikh. All these communities are there for reasons that are unique for them. [The question we have to ask is,] What is this entity who, known by different names, comes to everybody differently and has confused us all so much?'

We tried to find a quiet place to talk in the corner of the prayer hall but there was a great sense of activity around—people were getting the room ready for the evening hymn singing—so we moved to the corridor outside. This branch of Hinduism, Nitin told me, is simply 'a way to the Supreme Lord'.

'In my case I have found this road which is going to take me to the Creator.'

He told me how he joined the faith when he was eight, because of a very devoted mother. As a teenager, he says, he 'found the world' but then returned to the faith when he was about 38, since when he has been 'getting deeper and deeper in'.

Nitin had no difficulty in identifying the problems that spoil human life as greed and ego.

'Ego makes us want to be number one in everything. The only one that is number one is the Creator himself.'

One answer was to see that we have a lease on life, not a freehold.

'If you accept that the one thing that is absolutely definite is death and welcome it, then hopefully you become less possessive. I'm not saying that one should live life to look forward to death. I'm just saying one should live life to understand that it's illusion.

Then everything else becomes very easy. It's seeing things the way they are—that you're here for a particular purpose. One day the dream will break and you will say, "I wish I'd known."'

REDEMPTION AS THE GOAL

When I asked him about the goal of his religious life, Nitin said it was 'redemption'.

'You don't want to go through the cycles of life and death and you don't need to really. You want to reconnect with the Creator. Maybe "reconnect" is the wrong word: you want to be serving him. "Reconnect" implies you become part of him. In our philosophy we don't become part of God; we become like stars around the sun.'

'You mean it's more like a relationship,' I suggested.

'Yes, absolutely. That's what this is all about. People in my faith sometimes have a U shape with a red dot on their foreheads, [the U shape] meaning the Supreme Lord, and you as the dot, serving at his lotus feet constantly, surrounded by him, living with him. That's the goal.'

How certain was Nitin that he would reach this goal?

'Totally certain. There are two things that are certain: one is death and the other is the Supreme Being. We all go through the usual experiences that prove to us that things around us exist. The air that we breathe, the water that we drink, is certain, and these come from a source, which is the creator. So if the creator exists you should go to him. If you fail the exam you have to resit it: if you pass the exam you'll go to the highest realm.'

Might this take several lives?

'Yes, it depends on how I adapt to getting up the ladder, but the ladder does go in one direction, towards him. How do I know about that? I witness it in my Guru—the way he behaves—and in the things that happen, things of the spirit, not magical things but things that make you think there is something out there, that is making things happen in your own life. Everyone in my family has had unique experiences, things that make you believe that somebody is looking over your shoulder, especially when I'm in service for the Lord.'

Nitin offered to give me 'a small example' and I encouraged him.

'I've got lots of examples. In my computer is a section that says: "experiences that I've had that make me sure there is someone looking after me". This particular one proves two things, that the Lord lives through my Swami, my spiritual master, and that the Lord does exist.'

Nitin then told me about a trip he had organized for a party of monks to Paris. On the train on the way home he was sitting with his spiritual master and having a joke about why things had gone wrong on the way out.

'I said in a laughing way that when I'm doing voluntary work for the temple I always find that business goes up by ten per cent, and I said if the Lord can take over my business then I'm perfectly happy to be in his service. He laughed too and said, "But you should make sure you look after your office", which was a very strange comment for a Swami to make. As it happened I hadn't spoken to my office for 48 hours. So having heard this comment I borrowed a phone from somebody and phoned, and I'm glad I did. They'd been trying to get hold of me for the last 48 hours because I'd organized coaches to meet the train on the return leg, but I'd booked them for the wrong time. So there was the possibility of 400 people arriving in London with no transport. This phone call I'd now made saved me from this embarrassment.

'I feel that God is within me' (he continued). 'I hold his hand and I walk with him and he walks with me and as long as I'm holding it, his hand is always stretched out for me. He doesn't take his hand away. It's me that's silly enough to go away.'

PRAYER AS THE WAY TO PURITY

'Meditation is really to look within yourself, to your God, the spiritual stuff, but what that doesn't actually do is take your ego away. It's a great way of finding the Lord but it's not a purifier. What you need is a bar of soap which cleanses your soul and yoga doesn't quite do that either. It gives you peace of mind. It gives you a method of getting to the Lord, but not purity. Helping others and serving others should be normal behaviour but just because you help someone doesn't mean that you purify yourself either. Constantly praying and talking about the Lord reminds you of your witness, because seeing his purity reminds you of your impurity and helps you to purify yourself. So prayers and talking about the Lord is the best purifier there is.

'The easiest way to purify yourself is to stop yourself from having bad thoughts. An idle mind is the devil's workshop. So if your mind is constantly chanting the Lord's name, constantly, as you're walking, thinking, working, reading, eating, then it's no longer the devil's workshop. It's the Lord's.'

I asked Nitin about ritual and he said he thought there was a big difference between ritual and prayer.

'If you sit down in a nice five-star restaurant to have a great dinner, 100 per cent of what you do is ritual, ten percent is consuming food, which is like the religion. That's the difference between religion and ritual. If you take the ritual away, religion can become quite boring. Ritual is not religion. Your personal relationship with the Supreme is religion. Ritual is something that gives you a flavour so you stay religious.'

We began to talk about other religions.

'If the Lord wanted to have just one faith in this world he would have fixed it. If he wanted all of us to be the same colour he would have fixed it. I think he did what he did because he wanted to do it. In the same way that he accepts everyone's uniqueness and differences, we need to appreciate everyone's right to find their own path. Whether their path is the shortest way to heaven is not for me to determine.'

I asked him how he felt about sharing his faith with other people.

'You look at a jar of honey. You say, "Grr, it's lovely" and you offer [it to] a child to taste it, and that is the only way they can learn how useful it is.'

He went on to say that he was concerned how some people seem to believe that 'the only way is my way'.

'What we are saying then is, "My belief is superior to everybody else's", and one wonders to what degree one's ego is coming into this, one's pride. I cannot believe that the Lord God or a prophet would ever say that, and if they did it was appropriate for the time and the place where it was said, but not appropriate for the context of the world we live in today. That's one of the causes of the problems we have today, because the bottom line is, "My way is the best". That's what causes the rifts. It's the Lord's problem, and he'll sort it out, I'm sure.'

Nitin had had a phone call during the interview to remind him of a family event he was meant to be attending that evening. He suggested that I might like to stay to watch the Arati ceremony taking place soon, and left.

✢

I made a point of trying to meet women as well as men in each of the communities I contacted, because they often have a rather different perspective. Nitin arranged for me to come back to meet Shobhana Desai, the International Women's Coordinator for the Swaminarayan movement, who also works as a social worker for the local council. Swaminarayan, who started this sect of Hinduism in around 1800, was concerned about the position of women in Indian society and his solution was the separation of the sexes. He saw that women usually lost out when there was competition for leadership, so where he could he set up separate temples with the women completely in charge of every aspect of their own. The Swaminarayan movement has continued this tradition. Women sit in separate areas in the shrine and prayer rooms and run their own affairs.

When Shobhana took me to the women's section of administrative offices and meeting rooms, we passed a sign saying 'No gentlemen beyond this point'. She explained that the movement had expanded in Europe with temples in Paris, Lisbon, Milan and Vienna, and she is in constant contact with the head office in Amdavad in India. That evening she was expecting about 150 children and the next day, Sunday, over 600. A team of voluntary teachers and coordinators, trained and supervised by Shobhana, teach them the Gujarati language (which they use in their worship), about Indian culture in general and about Swaminarayan.

SHOBHANA DESAI

I asked Shobhana how she had become involved in the movement.

'That's very interesting because before marriage I didn't know anything about the Swaminarayan organization, but when I got married my husband's family were believers. I did have lots of

67

reservations. In my parents' house we believed in all the Hindu gods and then, when I came to join this family, it was very difficult for me to accept it. I did follow because it was a traditional family and as the elder daughter-in-law I followed whatever they said, but it didn't come from my heart. In 1979 I came over here with my husband. I didn't know anyone here so my involvement in the Swaminarayan sector was zero. But when the old temple in this road was being built in 1981, I started going and taking my children there. Then my husband fell ill. He was dying but he survived, with the blessing of our Guru, and my faith developed.'

Later Shobhana spoke more about this period of her life, but I went on to ask her how her faith made her life better. She began by saying that it was better for her daughters.

'If you see the difficulties people are having in today's society, [by] becoming Swaminarayan my daughters don't have those problems, like staying overnight away, the drugs, clubbing, everything. I'm not saying all these are bad things but they are sometimes diversions. For myself I don't know where I would be without it, because I have no relations in London but I have so many people here. If I have a problem, I know that people will be behind me. Spiritually I become stronger. An inside strength has developed. How can I describe the peace I get inside? Like, if any crisis comes in the family or anything, I know that for a couple of minutes I might get distressed but then I sit and think and I do get, very calmly, some solutions.'

The goal of her religious life was to become a good human being, but there was another aspect to it.

'Our goal is that after you are dead you will go to heaven. In our belief we go to the *Akshardham*, the place of our Lord, so you don't have to come back to go through the cycles of life and death. That is the main object, but to be a good citizen too—become a good mother or father or son or daughter. That is the goal—to serve the Lord, to become selfless, so you don't have any kind of self.'

She felt certain she would reach that goal when she looked at her past and saw the way she had developed.

'When I was young I was always arguing. "Is there a God? Show me there is a God!" I have developed by seeing things, by reading, by experiencing, and now I am very much certain that I will reach that goal. Only one example I can tell you—I'm not Gujarati by birth; I didn't have the Gujarati language. I have no relations here and yet I'm Coordinator of the International Women's Section. That is a big thing, isn't it? That's by the blessings of God.'

AN ANSWER TO PRAYER

Things Shobhana had read and things she had seen on visits to India had made her sure about her faith but so also had her own personal experiences, which, she told me, she had no hesitation in sharing with me.

'My husband was dying with cancer and the doctors gave up. They didn't even give him a time, they told us two hours, one day, any day, any time. The morning we were told he was dying, we had a letter from His Holiness Pramukh Swami Maharaj and it was only four lines, "Just continue the medication. You will be all right. Don't worry for your family here or there." The cancer specialist told us she couldn't do anything for him, just let him die. Then, because Pramukh Swami had written to continue the medication, we persuaded her to give him chemotherapy. She wasn't happy but she said she'd give him one dose and then a scan to see if there was any improvement. In the first week of January 1984 he had a scan and the cancer had disappeared. There wasn't any cancer and when she looked at the report she couldn't believe it. So that gave me very much faith. When it was announced in the temple, "this person is dying with cancer and he has a five-year-old and a one-year-old girl", in that evening everybody prayed and gave one day of their lives to my husband. That prayer worked and we believe that. It was God; who else could do it when the doctors were denying everything and he was dying? My husband is still surviving; he's doing very well. He's responsible for the welfare rights activity here.'

THE PRESENCE OF THE DIVINE

Shobhana told me that although you can't see God's power with your eyes, you can feel it.

'We believe in God's presence in Pramukh Swami Maharaj, and when I attend some ceremonies I do feel something divine actually inside to help me. Many other people have that faith also. So it's not something I have only experienced because my husband is alive. That's just one of the evidences that keeps my faith strong.'

When I asked her about her view of other religions, she told me that Pramukh Swami says no matter which religion you believe, you have to believe and trust in that and there is no need to change.

'It is not a kind of shop. At the end of the day when you're dying, then you call your Lord and he will come and help you. I come across Christian beliefs, with Christian colleagues and with people who come to my doorstep giving me the magazine *Awake*.[10] I do read it and some of the beliefs and some of the teachings are very good. When I take people around the exhibition [in the temple] I explain how the Lord said, "If someone has to have a lot of pain, give it to me, rather than to my disciple." So the teachings are similar. There's not a single religion that teaches all the good things. The only thing [that matters] is how much you believe and trust; how much faith you have. That is my personal opinion.'

✠

Bhaktivedanta Manor is set in a very different environment from the Swaminarayan temple. The elegant Victorian manor house, a few miles out of London, is surrounded by fields and woodland. It was donated to ISKCON, the International Society for Krishna Consciousness, by George Harrison in 1973. As well as meeting several of the resident monks, I was introduced to a most impressive team of oxen that help plough the land and give cart-rides to visiting schoolchildren. I saw the small primary school in action and was taken to the shop, where there were very tempting home-grown and home-baked goods for sale. Emerging from an ancient school of Hinduism, this movement, popularly known as 'Hare Krishna' because of their chant, was founded in 1965 in New York by Srila Prabhupada (1896–1977) to bring the wisdom of ancient India to the world.

I was shown around by Radha Mohan (born Richard Cole). Shoes came off outside the house and Radha was dressed in the familiar saffron robe. He told me there were 40 residents following monastic life in the temple. Services within the community include daily deity worship, and education, farm, mission and charity work of various kinds. Major festivals can draw up to 50,000 people.

RADHA MOHAN

Radha began by explaining what Hinduism is.

'To understand how we fit into what people call Hinduism, you have to understand what the word "Hindu" means. Generally it just means, "what is typical of ancient India". It's not one single easily definable religion, but at the same time, what unites Hindus are the ancient Vedic scriptures. The reason why there are so many forms of Hinduism is because the Vedas are so vast and are written at different levels for different people. We would differ from most other Hindu communities in that we are an international mission —a preaching, missionary movement, that has existed in an unbroken chain of Gurus and disciples going back at least five thousand years.'

The central figure for this movement is Krishna.

'Krishna is the form of God. We see God as having a personality, a form. Krishna means "the all-attractive Supreme Personality of Godhead". There are different names of God—Allah, Jehovah, Buddha and so forth—but we say this name best describes the personality of God.'

Also of great importance are their Gurus.

'Gurus, senior spiritual teachers, are important because they are connections between us and God. This society's principal Guru, Srila Prabhupada, is the most recent link of teachers in a tradition that can be traced back since time immemorial. He's where, in this particular tradition, we get our information about God. A lot of it is to do with faith and respect of the Guru.'

I asked Radha how these figures fitted in with the Hindu idea of incarnation.

'*Avatar* means "one who descends". God descends in different forms in this universe, on this planet. Krishna did come, but he is more than an *avatar*. We say Krishna is the original form of God, the equivalent to what Christians would call the Father, Almighty God.'

Radha had become involved in the movement when someone sold him a copy of the Bhagavad Gita *on the streets of Worcester. He read it when he*

was a student in Manchester a few years later and thought it was 'cool'.
He went on a tour of India and Europe arranged by the movement and on
the way back they stopped off at Bhaktivedanta Manor.

'I thought, OK. There's a small theatre group here and I'm an
actor. That was about nine years ago.'

A BETTER LIFE

I asked Radha how his faith made his life better, and he said it gave him
meaning, purpose, direction, and a sense of community.

'At the end of the day, if you believe in something it means
everything to you. It is your life. The purpose of your existence in
this life and where you go after this lifetime is defined by it.'

When I enquired about the problems of human life, he spoke about
suffering.

'We say that this world is a place of suffering. There's suffering
in this world because we all have to get older… disease, death,
that causes so much pain. There's suffering and anxiety, particularly if someone is materialistically minded. They try to be
happy and human society itself is trying to make people happy
through external reasons, without God, but this is actually
making things worse and making people feel more lost and sinful.
What Krishna Consciousness does is tell people how to be happy,
basically, both in this world and in the future. If people don't
know what they are, what the purpose of life is, then they are not
going to be happy. So we have to discover we are not the body, we
are consciousness, we are the soul.'

Radha explained that they want people to become Krishna conscious
so that they can return to the spiritual world as opposed to becoming
reincarnated.

'The goal of the individual is to achieve Krishna Consciousness. It would be a state of eternality, knowledge and bliss, without anxiety and full of love and beyond what we can imagine. Potentially both of us can reach it right now, or it can take millions of lifetimes, but it depends on us really. If someone has their arms round a large tree, they may say, "The oak tree won't let me go", but no, it's you that has to let go of this illusionary vision of the world. Eventually we all will reach this state. I'm very confident—eventually. For myself, let's say that if not this lifetime, maybe the next, or the next.'

These truths about how the world is had come to Radha through the writings of Srila Prabhupada and the classes and discussions they have at the temple.

'Without receiving information from a higher source, I don't know what's beyond this universe. There are those sources that are beyond the universe, so OK, how do we know they're true? It's faith. We talk about very ancient knowledge that hasn't changed over thousands of years. It's going back to God himself. He passes the information to a personality who passes it on to a personality on this earth.'

I asked him if it was something he experienced for himself.

'Yes, obviously there has to be something to keep me going. It's a self-experiential thing. You do feel more detached from this world. It's very gradual, though, like the opening of a flower. You become more aware of your soul, which is your actual identity, and more at peace with yourself. You begin to see the world in a different way.'

Did he, I asked him, feel he made contact with some spiritual reality outside himself?

'Yes, because you have to develop a relationship with Krishna and the Guru, who is a representative of Krishna. In the spiritual world the soul needs a relationship. I'm not a very high elevated personality so I'm not best mates with Krishna. He loves me. I don't love him, but I'm trying to work at that. Actually, when we do our meditation, which is the chanting of "Hare Krishna", we are inviting Krishna into our lives. When we chant "Hare Krishna" we're saying, "Oh all-attractive one, kindly engage me in your loving service." That's it, we're not saying, "Please give me a BMW and a cottage by the sea."'

HE ALWAYS ANSWERS

You're offering yourself in service?

'Yes. I don't think God is going to be interested in "please make me win the Lottery". As a child I tried prayers like that. What tends to happen in my experience is that prayers to Krishna are not answered when we ask for material things. It's only when we ask for spiritual things that he necessarily gives you the time of day. A miraculous thing is that when you genuinely pray to be spiritually connected, then he always answers.'

I asked him if, as a missionary movement, they wanted everyone to find this way.

'I don't see that we are the only way. It's more like, say you're going from Birmingham to London—it may be pretentious, but we would think of ourselves as the motorway route. We shouldn't have a sectarian view of things, but we are confident that we are the fastest way to get back to God.'

Radha didn't think God could be limited to one religion.

'God is God. These different religions are different expressions of worshipping him. They have emerged at different periods of history but we have to go beyond these different designations.'

He thought it was a mistake to become attached to your religion as the only way.

'There are people who say Jesus is the only way. At the end of the day you have to focus on Jesus' saying, "I am the way, the truth and the life". What do we say to that? We say, "What is the way? What is the truth?" The truth is to love God with all your mind and heart and soul. So Jesus' way *is* the only way, but he's teaching "love God", and we're doing that as well. We don't really think Jesus was teaching a sectarian philosophy. I think we have to get closer to Jesus, but we would say there are other personalities who taught God consciousness that are just as valid.'

The Hindus I had met so far, from the Swaminarayan and ISKCON movements, were from what might be called theistic traditions within Hinduism. At a meeting of the London Interfaith Centre in Kilburn, I met Jay Lakhani. He was taking part in an evening called 'Understanding Hinduism'. He began his talk by saying that self-centred spirituality was a perfect oxymoron, a complete contradiction in terms. Where self-interest appears, he suggested, spirituality disappears. If you seek your own salvation, you sink. It is only in learning to live for others that true spirituality is to be found.

JAY LAKHANI

When we met later, we found a quiet spot in a Hindu temple nearby and Jay explained that his enthusiasm, information and inspiration came from two very recent figures in Hinduism, Ramakrishna (1834–86) and Vivekananda (1863–1902). He explained:

'About ten years ago, I felt that I had enough financial support to spend the rest of my life doing what I really enjoy, so I decided to retire from my business activities and focus on the thing that I love, which is spirituality. I started with very small classes—about half a dozen youngsters coming to learn about Hinduism. The classes are non-sectarian and non-commercial. I'm not starting a new Vivekananda cult but trying to explain the most comprehensive aspects of Hinduism to Hindu youngsters as well as the Hindu community and the host nation. The majority of my time is spent talking about Hinduism to Western youngsters. I go to a great many schools, to colleges and universities, talk to lots of RE teachers. I'm involved in publications and so on.'

I asked him about his earlier life and he told me that he was born in East Africa.

'My family left India three generations back, settled in East Africa for a couple of generations and I came here as a young boy of 15. My parents were interested in more traditional Hindu forms, but there was definitely an inclination to spiritual matters.'

I asked him my central question about how his faith made his life better.

'There are two aspects. Suppose you want more money or flashy cars or lots of holidays, you might then feel satisfied with that and that is the end of the matter, because you don't need really to look for spirituality. Hinduism allows for that; it says, unless you go through that phase, spirituality cannot dawn at all. The hope is that you mature out of it and then get drawn to spiritual matters.'

Then, he told me, things can start to change.

'The same things that you saw in a secular way, you now see in a spiritual way. You have the same daily routine but now the way you view the world and yourself can become dramatically different.

This is how spirituality helps us in our daily lives because in a way it invokes greater love of life itself—because you are now drawing not from secular objectives but from spiritual objectives, and you seem to be fulfilling a greater need.'

Again he thought of the problems of the world in terms of suffering.

'We all face the same problem, which is suffering. It's very difficult to reconcile suffering with spiritual teachings—the fact that you see people, perhaps for no fault of their own, go through a life of misery, literally living at the level of animals. If you look at the animal kingdom you see tremendous ferocity and vicious-ness. It makes you wonder. How can one bring oneself to believe that there is a merciful God behind this universe?'

THE NON-DUALISTIC PHILOSOPHY OF HINDUISM

So what sort of answers did his faith give to this problem?

'My answer says that, really, what you see is the world of appear-ances, not reality, so it's necessary to see through an apparent world, to reach out and touch something grander that underlies it. So my answer is, suffering and pleasure do not really exist. There is something higher, at a deeper level that transcends both of them.'

How could a philosophy like that be translated into daily life? Jay said it was difficult.

'I grow my strength from the findings of modern physics, because there you suddenly come across an explanation of what the world is all about. It says that, really, the world is not as it appears. It is not made out of sticks and stones or smaller versions of sticks or stones. There is something far greater, which is transcendent and yet very necessary to explain this manifested universe, and even if the manifestations appear extremely real, they are not reality; they are a secondary phenomenon. This is the non-dualistic philosophy of Hinduism.'[11]

Jay told me that, in a way, this philosophy is not very satisfying because it may seem to be an escapist route that just denies both pleasure and pain, but once you realize that this world is a secondary phenomenon, you realize that it can never really answer primary questions. In order for you to find a primary answer, you need to dig deeper into the nature of reality, your own nature and the nature of this universe.

He found the philosophy of Shankara (788–822) 'very lovely' and told me one of his stories.

'Shankara is saying: this is the world of appearance and there is something higher. So the king listened to the story, which sounded very philosophical, and then while the king was watching, there came a cry, "Wild elephant coming, run, run!" And Shankara ran like nobody's business, the elephant rushing behind him, and very quickly climbed up a tree and escaped. The elephant went away. Shankara came down and went to the king. The king was laughing his head off. He said, "Now, Shankara, you said this was the world of appearance, so why did you run?" Look at the answer of Shankara! This gives the heart of non-dualistic philosophy. He said, "O king, the fact that you saw me flying up the tree was also appearance."

'In order to get rid of a disease which is an appearance, you need to adopt a medicine that is also an appearance. This is the way he gets out of a very difficult theological problem. How do we explain suffering or difficulty? The best answer I find is in a very ancient philosophy, but it's one that finds an ally at the heart of physics and this gives me the greatest support.'

A NEW IDEA ABOUT SALVATION

When we began to talk about a goal in his life, Jay told me of a new idea in Hinduism.

'In ancient times, to reach the goal of religion it was considered necessary to go off in solitude and search for God, to find your own salvation, but a more recent, contemporary approach to spirituality comes from Vivekananda, who says this is wrong. By doing that, you are in fact ignoring the greatest store of spirituality, which is mankind. Interacting with people is the best way to generate spirituality. It is a universal rather than a personal search. It's not for my salvation; it's for everyone's salvation that you play this game—of talking spirituality, invoking spirituality, not just in yourself but in others. Looking for individual salvation is perhaps itself a selfish motivation. Bringing religion or spirituality alive in the whole of the community or society is the goal. Your goal as an individual is to erase the ego.'

I asked him if he could give me a definition of what he meant by spirituality.

'What we have studied all our lives has been a secondary phenomenon, studied with another secondary phenomenon—the physical world, as reflected in the mind—and we try to make sense of the world and live through that. What we need is to develop the maturity to see that there is something far grander underlying this universe that we thought was very mundane—something very vibrant.'

Was this something that he not only believed in but also experienced?

'Spiritual experience is not something that someone else can have and you just refer to it. You have to have it for yourself, and that makes religion really come alive. A great deal of emphasis is placed on personal spiritual experience. It's not something that you just believe in; it is something that you can experience for yourself. Unless it was so, I would lose interest in it, but this is a very personal thing and it's not recommended that it should be discussed in public, or [written about] in books.'

PRAYER AND WORSHIP

When I asked him about prayer and worship, Jay said he was perhaps the worst Hindu I could have come across in this respect.

'I do not follow any particular ritual or daily routine; I do not sit for meditation; I do not worship on a daily basis.'

So how was he pursuing this spirituality?

'In this way of interacting with human beings. I find that more vibrant and exciting than sitting down and closing my eyes and thinking about God. You see, I go to schools and I see lots of youngsters. I'm very much in my element because I like human beings. So I do my worship, my ritual, by interacting with other human beings.'

I introduced the question of other religions, and Jay said that he did not intend it as a compromising or patronizing statement but from what he knew of Christ he could say without the slightest hesitation that there was nothing he had found in his teachings that he couldn't agree with wholeheartedly.

'I have found them very vibrant [in terms] of spirituality. Hindus have nothing to disagree with as far as the teachings of Christ are concerned, but they have a great deal to say regarding the Church. Let me give you an example. The teachings of Christ that I can relate to very easily are his two-pronged attack on greed and lust—but then you see the Vatican running banks; you see Christian priests asking to marry and, if they don't, they get up to serious mischief. The teachings of Christ are not quite coming true; lust and greed seem to be running the show. It is worrying for the Hindu.'

MISSIONARY ZEAL

'The second aspect is this missionary zeal that Christians seem to feel is necessary. It was one thing for Christ to say, "Go and explain this religion to others!" This message was given two thousand years ago. Now we live in a world where there are lots of other vibrant religions that coexist with Christianity. So if you try and insist on this now, you are going to produce sharp edges to your religion, which are going to come into conflict with other religions. To what extent can you continue your missionary zeal when you recognize other very valid, very vibrant, religious traditions?

'The idea of conversion, for the Hindu, is absolute perversion. Various groups of people throughout history, in different parts of the world, have followed their own traditions and have developed spirituality in their own mould, in a way that appealed to them and has become part and parcel of their life. It's very foolish to ask them to switch religions.'

SOME REFLECTIONS

You may have noticed as you listened to these people talking that, although there were enormous differences in what they believed and how they practised their religion (and these differences don't begin to represent the variety you can find within Hinduism), there were some common themes running through them. One of the things that sticks in my mind from this series of visits is the practice of removing one's shoes, as a symbol of entering a place that was different—a practice that I discovered was common to all the religions with the exception of Judaism and Christianity.

Did you notice the references to reincarnation, to belief in the Vedas as 'ancient knowledge' that comes from God himself, and the idea that God comes to us in different ways—Swami Narayan as an incarnation of the Supreme Being, and Krishna as 'the original form of God' who came to the world? One aspect that I found most interesting was the way the ego, the self, loomed large as the problem, and the idea that the answer lies somehow in seeing things differently. Nitin said, 'Once you understand that life is illusion, everything else becomes very easy.' To Radha the answer was discovering what you are: 'If people don't know what they are, what the purpose of life is, they are not going to be happy.' Jay told me it was a matter of seeing the world differently. What we needed was 'to reach out and touch' the spiritual reality that underlies the apparent world

Another way of taming the ego, that we will see again in later chapters, was to try to centre the mind on God, by constantly chanting the Lord's name or repeating a prayer of self-offering.

All the people in this section believed that their faith was something that they experienced for themselves. There was Nitin who said, 'This creator who comes to people in different forms and different names, gives people experiences', and who always finds God's hand when he reaches for it; Shobhana who could see God working in her life and believes that prayer works; Radha who said, 'The miraculous thing is that when you genuinely pray to be spiritually connected, then he always answers'; and Jay who told me that personal spiritual experience was what kept him interested, but it was 'a very personal thing', not for writing in books. To the theistic Hindus this was the experience of a relationship that would continue for eternity.

Nitin's remarks about ritual interested me too and we will hear more later about the place it has in other people's lives. Perhaps typically of Hindus, these four all found it quite hard to relate to the idea that one religion could be the only way. Nitin felt that God had created differences for a reason and that we should accept them too. Jay's question, 'To what extent can you continue your missionary zeal, when you recognize other very valid, very vibrant religious traditions?' is one that stayed with me.

CHAPTER 7

LISTENING TO JEWS

The London Borough of Barnet has a high concentration of Jewish people living within its boundaries. The Sternberg Centre for Judaism is in our parish and I could walk to a dozen or more synagogues and Jewish schools of many different varieties. My first conversation was with Nicola Goldsmith, a friend and business partner of my daughter. Nicola is married to the rabbi at the Liberal Synagogue in North Finchley. They send their children to the Church of England primary school that my grandchildren attend and her husband sometimes takes the morning assembly there.

NICOLA GOLDSMITH

I arrived at Nicola's home as they were finishing their evening meal. After banishing her husband from the room, she told me that she 'was brought up Liberal', in Dulwich, where Jewish people were very much in the minority.

I asked her to explain what was characteristic about Liberal Judaism and she told me that Orthodox Jews aim to live within detailed rules that are laid down by their rabbinic hierarchy. The Torah says, for example, that you shouldn't kindle a fire on Sabbat, and the modern ruling would be that, by analogy, you can't turn on a light.

'Liberal Judaism is different in that you go back to the original text and you see that the reason it says you shouldn't kindle a fire on Shabbat is because it's meant to be a day of rest, when you're not working. When that was written, lighting a fire would have been quite a lot of work, but switching on a light is no effort, so that's not contrary to the principle of rest. Our interpretation would be that you shouldn't go to work. It should be a day that's different. There are a lot of texts you can go back to [for guidance], but you're free; you're encouraged to question and you don't all come to the same conclusion. Some people [in our community] keep Sabbat, some don't. Some people keep kosher,[12] some don't. We keep a vegetarian and fish kitchen at the synagogue so as not to upset those people who have made the choice [to keep kosher], but that's entirely a personal thing—we don't.'

The Torah is very important to Liberal Jews but it is not the only text they refer to.

'There are three thousand years' of writings including the Talmud and the Mishna. Particularly in the Liberal movement, 100 to 150 years ago there were some really key thinkers who've left absolutely fantastic legacies of thoughts and prayers and sermons that are all available for us to use as source texts, and they're equally inspirational.'

When I asked Nicola about her role in the synagogue, she said that she tries very hard not to be simply a rabbi's wife. They've had women rabbis in Liberal synagogues for over 30 years and people no longer expect to employ one person and get two.

'I have my own role. I was very involved in Liberal Judaism before I met Mark. I had my own route in, my own identity, long before he came along. It's his work and I don't want to influence things, but I do run the monthly kindergarten, which is an educational one. I have been known to sit on the odd committee and we have a presence. We are there. I think it's important for the children to feel an ownership of the place.'

A BETTER LIFE?

I asked Nicola how her faith made her life better.

'The whole concept of biblical Judaism is actually, to me, a culture, a community. It's a very humanistic religion and essentially if you are just a little bit better, just a little bit kinder, thoughtful, generous, and you can encourage everyone else around you to do the same, then you are going to live in a slightly better world. That is what it means to me. My structure for that comes from Judaism because that's what I've been brought up with. It teaches you about justice and fairness and to be critical. Family values are massively important. For example, it was my grandmother's 92nd birthday. Twenty-eight of the family were there. I'm sure that if we hadn't all been brought up Liberal Jewish, coming together [for] Seder night, New Year, Rosh Hashanah, we wouldn't be such a close-knit family. These values are reinforced a lot in the liturgy all the time.'

After a pause she added:

'I don't know what life would be like without it. I was so immersed in it from day dot. I have never known a life without it, so I couldn't possibly say.'

There were various goals in Nicola's religious life. She reminded me that she had already talked about the goal of living in a responsible way, making the world a better place, but she could see that you could equally well say this as a humanist, and there was another strong motivation in her life that came directly from her Jewishness.

'I feel a massive responsibility to ensure that Judaism lives. We were almost, almost finished off and that really wasn't very long ago. When you see there are only 300,000 Jews left in the UK and there are hardly any in the rest of Europe, I feel a massive weight of responsibility to try to ensure that it exists, but actually I'm not convinced it will. I think Hitler will get his way in the end, very sadly. Six million Jews was just too many. I feel that as a responsibility for those of us who are left, even though both my parents' families had moved out of Germany before [the war began], so it isn't all that direct.

'Being Jewish gives you an extraordinary connection with this historical event and we're just getting to the stage now where the last survivors are dying off and it's really quite frightening. It's silly things like realizing the difference in teaching between what we learn from a Jewish background [and] what the kids learn in school. Things are glossed over, as were the Crusades and all the other times when there was Jewish persecution. Lovingly they stick a plaster over it all, which means people are not learning.'

I asked Nicola if she could separate out the race, the culture and the religion, but she said:

'It's so connected, I'm not sure that I can make the distinction. It's all one massive package.'

Did she want it to survive because Judaism was good for the world?

'Yes, I think it is it. It's so sensible. We don't convert anybody, we don't put pressure on anybody. We say, "Let's understand everybody else's culture and embrace it." I don't think it's any better than anything else necessarily, but I do think the world would be a much, much poorer place without it.'

Nicola had this additional goal in life because of her Jewishness, but how did Liberal Judaism, as a religion, actually differ from humanism?

'There's this great lump of history. There's all the culture, the ritual. I'm very involved in it. Look at this place! [Her living room was full of Jewish artefacts of one sort or another.] I think that's what people cling to and I think that's what has kept Judaism alive through generation after generation of persecution. You've had to be able to pick up your religion and move at the drop of a hat. What can you take with you? A few artefacts and your book.'

I wanted to get on to the question of spirituality within Judaism, so I asked her if God was someone she felt she could contact or get to know.

'I think you'd get a different answer for every Jew you talked to. It's not like being a Christian; you can be a very committed and dedicated Jew and not believe in God. I think it's accepted that, as you go through your life, you're probably going to dip in and out of the whole concept of spirituality. There's a lot there for you as a Liberal Jew if you want to uncover your spiritual background or investigate it but there's no difficulty or embarrassment about having an integral part in community life if you're not at a stage in your life when [spirituality's] actually relevant. I've dipped in and out in my life and I'm sure I shall continue to do so. At the moment Mark has enough spirituality for both of us, but it might change. I have no problem with that.'

CELEBRATING 'YOM KIPPUR'

Nicola then went on to tell me that Yom Kippur (the Day of Atonement) was the time in the year when most Jewish people felt most contact with their spiritual side, and how she felt some resentment that, with two small children, she can't experience Yom Kippur as she used to.

'I can't sit in the synagogue from 11 o'clock in the morning till 8 o'clock at night because they have needs and I run the kindergarten, and I do miss it because it used to be enough for me for a year. It's very intense. It's something that I think an awful lot of people would benefit from. When you're feeling, "Stop the world, I want to get off", it gives you that 24 hours to ask yourself:

Now who am I? Why am I that person? Why do I respond to situations like I do? Why is the world as it is? What have I done in the last year that was right, that was wrong, that could have been better? How can I improve my self-knowledge such that I can grow from it? It's terribly intense and very, very refreshing.'

Could you not do that sort of self-reflection on your own?

'Yes, you can, but there's something very extraordinary about being in a room with hundreds of people doing it all together. Some of it is structured and the prayers lift you through the day, in and out of thinking about yourself, the community and the world. It's very cleverly designed so that you think both about the past and about the future. A piece of music is played at the bringing in of *Yom Kippur* and it is most extraordinarily poignant. It's usually sung or played on a cello and all I need to do is hear that! It's about being an individual, but you're an individual within a very large group of people, and there's something incredibly powerful about that. No, I don't think you can do it on your own. It's just not the same. There's something great about sitting there all day and thinking, not only are you there in a room with 200 [or] 300 people, but in every other synagogue in London, in the UK, in the world, on that day, everybody is doing the same thing, and has been for thousands of years.

'*Yom Kippur* tends to be the day that brings out Jews who aren't very involved in Judaism for the rest of the year. It isn't guilt. We don't do guilt—except possibly if your mother doesn't make very good chicken soup. No matter how strong or weak your identity is, it's the one thing in the year that is likely to make you think, "That's where I come from. I want to be part of it," even though it's the most solemn day in the Jewish calendar.'

Nicola said she had 'fleeting problems' with prayer, but her mother, who was not spiritual at all, had been determined, particularly because they were living in a very non-Jewish world, that her children should understand the concept of prayer within Judaism. With her own children Nicola said:

'I feel I am arming them through prayer and education, that actually being Jewish is OK, and it can bring something to your life and through that you can bring something to the world.'

She had told me earlier that her little girl of five had been upset by teasing about being Jewish at school that day. She hoped that prayer might give them the skills to be resilient with things like that.

'I [faced] a huge amount of hostility in my school, but not as much as my brothers did. They really suffered.'

FAITH SCHOOLS

I was interested in Nicola's decision to send her children to an Anglican school and she told me:

'Mark and I have very strong opinions about single-faith schools. We would never in a million years send our children to a Jewish school. We just think they're wrong. Christian schools are different. We live in a Christian country, and Christian schools, unless they're Catholic, don't exclude other religions. We wanted very much to bring up our children within other groups of families where religion actually matters. It might be tough on the surface but in the end our children will identify much better with that. In fact, one of the things that we're particularly interested in at the moment is a move within Christian, Muslim and Jewish groups to set up a faith secondary school, which would be fabulous. It would be full of children who have religion as part of their life, but live in a multicultural environment.'

I asked Nicola if she felt her religion represented the truth and whether she was concerned that other people should accept it too.

'It's true for me. Actually I have very strong feelings about this and I expect this is quite a Jewish feeling. There's been so much persecution and so much forced conversion. I think one should only be acting within a religion if that really is the religion for you. I don't believe in the concept of saving other people's souls. I can't do that! The core of Liberal Judaism is about tolerance, understanding, knowledge, live and let live, welcoming the stranger; it's totally and utterly contrary to the teachings we live by to think that we could convert everyone around us because our way is the "right" way. It's *a* right way, and I think it's a very powerful, sane, very humanistic way.'

Finding an Orthodox Jew to talk to turned out to be more problematic. Eventually, through the Interfaith Centre in Kilburn, I found an Anglican clergyman involved with the Council of Christians and Jews, who suggested that I contact Vernon Mark, an enthusiastic member of the Council and also of the Orthodox Synagogue in West Hampstead. Vernon, who had worked in interior design up to the time of his retirement, was reluctant to talk to me, saying that he wasn't a very orthodox Jew, but he was persuaded and I visited him at his home in Wembley on a rare sunny day in January.

VERNON MARK

After making me tea and offering me chocolate cake and coconut biscuits, Vernon sat down to talk with me. He wanted to begin by telling me why he was committed to the Council of Christians and Jews, which he became a member of 'a very long time ago'. It was a story that went back to his childhood in Germany.

'By whatever one might like to call it, providence perhaps, an English Christian lady offered to look after this Jewish boy. She didn't speak any German and she had met my brother for precisely one week, because he happened to be the best friend of the son of a Jewish woman whom this lady had got to know. When this Christian lady, who had four grandchildren of her own, retired down to Worthing, in Sussex, she spoke to her Jewish friend and said, "Maybe your son would like to come down for a week by the seaside." The boy said, "Yes, please, and can I bring a friend?" and that [friend] happened to be my brother. With just that short acquaintance with my brother, the lady, when she heard of my circumstances, said, "Oh, I'll look after him."'

Vernon then explained what the circumstances were. His parents were living in Germany and their names were on the waiting list to emigrate to a number of countries.

'It was a time of considerable unemployment all over the world. Countries said, "You can come, but you've got to go on a waiting list. We can only absorb so many immigrants per annum." It was 1938; my parents were anxious that I should leave as soon as possible. Things were getting very difficult. I left in the evening after *Kristallnacht*—the night when synagogues and Jewish businesses were destroyed by the Nazis. That morning my father had been taken away. He'd had a call from somebody warning him, "I should go out if I were you. They are rounding people up." So he went out. The police came and gave strict orders that he was to report when he got back. I left that evening. My mother took me the first part of the way. It must have been awful for her, on reflection. I don't know if I was aware of it at the time, because I was eleven and off on a great adventure. Her husband had been taken away that morning and her boy was going off into another country and she didn't know when she would see him again. In fact, we didn't see each other again.'

The war broke out the following year, but Vernon was safe.

'The Christian lady looked after me very well. A cousin of hers, who also came to live in Worthing during the war, said to her, "You ought to get that boy converted!" but she responded, "Certainly not. I'm *in loco parentis* and that's not what his parents would have wished."'

What she did instead was to introduce him to the local Jewish community.

'During the war there was a tiny Jewish congregation in Worthing with no regular rabbi. They held services in a church hall where there was a cupboard that they used as the Ark. I had my *bar mitzvah* there.'

YOU DON'T HAVE TO BE THE CHIEF

Vernon had been thinking about what he was going to say to me, and the next thing he wanted to tell me was something he had heard as a teenager, that he felt had moulded his development and still influenced his participation in religious life. One young man returned to Worthing after his National Service and, before going to Oxford, set up a small Jewish youth club. There were about six regular members, from early teens upwards, and they met regularly on Saturday afternoons.

'It was during this time that I came across the words of a famous rabbi who lived about AD100. They were recorded in *The Ethics of the Fathers*. He said something like, "You are not expected to finish the task, but neither are you free to desist from it." You all have to do your bit, in other words. When this guy went off to university, it was left to the rest of us to carry on with this club, and I did my bit. Later on I helped the congregation in the ways I could. I took the minutes of the board meetings, things like that. This is something that has stayed with me—you don't have to be the chief; Indians are required as well.'

There was something else too that inspired his religious life.

'Of course, the other thing is that I was born a Jew and in view of what the Nazis' object was, I'm jolly well going to be a Jew. I've never tried to go into the matter of the Holocaust to the extent of asking, "Why didn't God intervene?" Someone said, "It wasn't God who did it, but man. Never mind 'where was God?' Where was man?"'

I asked him about the synagogue he now attended.

'It's part of the United Synagogue of which the Chief Rabbi is the head. I went to this particular synagogue when I lived in lodgings near Finchley Road station. This was the nearest one and I got to like it very much. It had an interesting rabbi, a cantor with a very good voice and a mixed choir, which in those days was acceptable within the United Synagogue but a few years later definitely went out. There are times now when, in my head, I can still hear that choir. It's a beautiful building and it was very formal when I first went. Eighty per cent of the men must have worn black jackets, striped trousers and bowler hats. It's all much more relaxed now.'

I asked him if he held any role at the synagogue.

'While I worked for a company, I couldn't go, during the winter, to Friday night services. Once I started working for myself I said, "Well, it's your choice now. You can probably organize yourself so that you can attend." Certain prayers need a minimum of ten men above the age of 13. So I'm doing my bit. I make sure that if I'm in Britain, I'll be there.'

There was, he told me, a considerable limit to his participation in synagogue matters but he did feel he had a role in welcoming visitors and newcomers. He felt he was ill-equipped for studying but was sometimes asked to give a resumé of the weekly reading from the five books of Moses, and he enjoyed preparing and presenting that, because it made him give more attention to the passage.

Practising Judaism had made his life better because he found he was in agreement with a great many of the rules for how one should conduct oneself in life.

'There are all sorts of strict regulations about this, that and the other, but human life comes first and you can break the rules—of Sabbath, for instance—to save a life. I thoroughly approve of one day in a week being different. When I was at a Jewish youth club I knew that a lot of the people on the board used to phone each other on a Friday night when they were sure their colleagues would be at home. One man refused to answer his phone on a Friday night and the older I got, the more I thought, excellent! [Having] one day different means that you make room for other things, which you don't when every day is exactly the same. And we started it!'

Vernon found that he was, in the same way, in agreement with the reasons underlying some of the festivals.

'When you're a child, you look forward to fasting on *Yom Kippur*. After the first two or three years, you realize it wasn't such a great thing to look forward to, but food is not everything, and you're meant to apologize to anybody you've offended during the year. The rest of it is between you and God. There are lots of things in my life that I am going to need a great deal of forgiveness for, but let's hope that I can ask God, "Well, why did you make me that way? This wasn't my choice."'

When I asked him about the goal of his life, he told me that he didn't have a specific one beyond living an ethical life and participating in the life of the synagogue.

'I don't feel that, as far as my religion is concerned, I must achieve this or that before I go off.'

HOPES BEYOND DEATH

Did he have any hopes beyond death?

'Religiously, no. I can't say that I do, which might be lazy of me. Maybe I could have expanded my activities. Maybe I have a view of my own abilities which hasn't stretched them as much as they should have been.'

Did he feel God was someone he could get to know?

'That is the most difficult thing of all. A young friend who has become very orthodox asked me something like that, and I said, "I don't know and I won't know until I die." When you read about the floods in Bangladesh, the droughts in Africa and the horrendous consequences of earthquakes, all the results of natural phenomena, at that point you do wonder about God, but I don't want to tackle that until I have to.'

Do you believe that you will meet God when you die, and all will become clear?

'I don't know that *all* will become clear, but at least his existence will. I hope he's there. I expect him to be much more understanding about certain human behaviour than other human beings. I hope, I trust he will be there.'

He was very positive about prayer, however.

'Some prayers in Jewish services reflect on the customs in the temple when the sacrifices were made—horrendous as far as I am concerned! However, I think it's lovely to say thank you to God for the first fruits in season. I don't buy strawberries in winter. I like seasons. On the first night of festivals we say, "Thank you for enabling me to reach this season."'

Vernon told me that certain prayers at certain times were more reflective and more personal.

'The prayers at *Yom Kippur* draw your attention to something else in your life. The odd psalm is rather nice too, whether it's in synagogue or set to music by Handel. I like the prayer that is said on the anniversary of someone's death—prayers that celebrate and commemorate? Yes!'

Wanting to go back to the subject of the temple sacrifices, Vernon told me that he had been asked to speak about such a passage one Sabbath, and he reminded the congregation that when someone does something at a cost to themselves, but totally for the benefit of someone else, the expression still used is that they have 'made a sacrifice'. When I asked him about the idea of a sacrifice that could atone for sin, however, he said:

'No, no. If you've done some damage to someone else, for heaven's sake try and put it right, as best you can, but not at the expense of an animal.'

Vernon told me that he was very at ease with other faiths. He had a Buddhist monk who was a friend and came to stay, and he had once been godparent to a Christian child. I asked him if there were people at the synagogue who might not think that a good idea. He said there might be some and added, 'Mind you, the vicar didn't think it was a good idea either!'

He then told me about the time he was invited to a cathedral when a friend of his was consecrated as a bishop.

'I reckon I was probably the only Jewish person there. I stayed in my seat when they went forward to celebrate the eucharist. The woman next to me said briskly, "Aren't you coming along?" I said I wasn't a Christian and she said, "Oh well, you might as well come and get the blessing", but I thought that would be cheating.'

As I left, Vernon invited me warmly to visit his synagogue any Saturday morning and bring a group of students if I wanted to. I had enjoyed my time with him so much that I definitely felt I might.

✣

One of my closest friends at church, whose husband is Jewish, showed me an article about a local rabbi in the *Jewish Chronicle*. Rabbi Jonathan Wittenberg is the leader of the New North London Synagogue, the largest synagogue in the Masorti tradition. He had recently written a manifesto[13] for this, Britain's youngest synagogue movement. I phoned and he was happy for me to come to his home for an interview.

Both the synagogue and the rabbi's house are in our parish, so I was able to walk, through freshly fallen snow, to his home. There was evidence of children and a dog and a rabbit, wonderful houseplants taking over the living-room and a view of a much-loved garden, sprinkled with snow. The rabbi made me tea and settled with the dog at his feet. I asked him about the Masorti movement.

RABBI JONATHAN WITTENBERG

The word Masorti *is Hebrew for 'traditional', and Rabbi Wittenberg said:*

'What makes it feel like the right home for me is the traditional liturgy and practice of Judaism which I grew up with and have always loved, and the openness to truth, wherever it comes from. There's the ability to understand Judaism as it's developed, as it is in relation to the modern world, to be deeply committed to it and yet at the same time very open.'

I asked him where it stood within the spectrum of Judaism and he told me it was roughly in the middle.

'It has a strong emphasis on tradition and observance, in Jewish terms the *Halakhah*. The key doctrine which is different from Orthodoxy is the way we understand the Torah as "from heaven". We understand the Torah as revealed through history, as the way people have tried to understand God's will, but we don't understand it literally as though it was dictated, and that leaves a greater flexibility of interpretation. We include insights from history and archaeology in the way we understand the very root sources of our Judaism. We see Judaism as a developing religion right from the start.'

I then asked him about his own, personal journey.

'The rabbinate is probably in my blood: from both sides it's quite a tradition. My mother's father was a rabbi in Frankfurt and escaped at the last moment. His father before him was an Orthodox rabbi, also in Germany. My father's mother came from a family which is a line of Orthodox rabbis, so that has given me a great love of traditional Judaism.'

Rabbi Wittenberg thought his faith made his life better in a number of different ways, giving him a structure, a community, a sense of values and opportunities for finding God's presence.

'On the most basic level it gives my life a structure in terms of time—the day and its prayers; the week and its Sabbath; the year and its festivals. So I feel I belong to a much greater rhythm, an ancient, rich way of life, and it gives my life a context within a community. One of the most painful things people suffer is a sense of sheer isolation. In the community there is a great feeling of togetherness, spiritual togetherness, but also social together-ness, especially for the children.

'[Judaism teaches me] to do what is meaningful and worth-while and that's very much connected to a sense of values that emphasize care, sensitivity, lasting commitment, the appreciation of the sanctity of the world. So there isn't really a day or an hour when one can't find something worthwhile to do, and that's very important in a world that can feel very dissociated from a sense of direction.

'Spiritually I'm surrounded with opportunity, the whole time. Sometimes I don't take it as much as I would wish, but there is constant opportunity in prayer life, opportunity in study life. For the Jewish person, studying the Torah is one of the routes to finding God's presence. I have joy studying Hasidic and mystical teaching. The emphasis there is very much on spirit and feeling and I find that very sustaining and engaging.'

When I asked him about the goal of his religious activities, he wanted to divide it into his personal goal and his goal as a rabbi.

'Personally, my goal is to live as good, as caring a life as I can, as much of the time as I can. Spiritually—hopefully to develop a sustaining sense of the spirit, strong enough to guide me through life's bad times as well as life's good times. As a rabbi—to try and share with others and encourage us all to support one another in that endeavour, as well as to be aware of the Jewish traditions, of the great resource we have there.'

The rabbi's booklet about Masorti Judaism affirms Judaism as a way of life 'rooted in faith in the one God as revealed in the Torah, the Bible and subsequent history'. 'The beaten path of Jewish life and teaching,' he had written, 'can help us find God.' [14] *So I asked him if that goal would involve developing a relationship with God.*

'Yes, that would be fine,' he said, and then, after some hesitation:

'For me it's a relationship with God through the life around me, an awareness of a relationship with God through people and their interactions, through nature especially, through prayer and texts certainly; but it's the sense of respecting and finding God's immanence in all those areas of life, which makes me prefer to put it that way, not suggesting that it's something different and other than the rest of life.'

How confident was he that he would reach his goal?

'I don't know what "reach" means here. It's a constant striving. There isn't a place of attainment. The end is death and the challenge is to live the whole of life, up to and including the end, as well as possible.'

Was there any goal beyond death?

'Yes, maybe, but that is beyond me. I can do the best I can living here and that's my challenge.'

So does he feel he makes contact with some spiritual reality?

'Yes, occasionally. I don't want to exaggerate it. It seems to me that it's something quite special and privileged: we don't have a right to it and I would make no claims to being constantly and regularly aware of life at that level, but I think it is always there and sometimes I do feel a small awareness of it.'

I asked him how he thought these truths had come to him, and he said he felt there were two parts to the process.

'One is the part of tradition, mediated by generation after generation of ancestors, through the way they have lived, through the texts, writings, traditions, laws of Judaism, and they really are guidance towards ethical and spiritual dimensions of life. The other route is universal, the privilege to live alongside people, in nature, through the resources of the spirit that are available to us all. Ultimately I don't experience a contradiction between what [those two parts] tell me.'

PRAYER AND STUDY

Prayer and ritual, worship and meditation, were all important to Rabbi Wittenberg.

'Prayer [is something I do] regularly. It is a discipline. Sometimes the gates open, sometimes they don't; but I consider regular prayer extremely important because, like any other activity, if I don't do it regularly, how can I expect it to really resonate?'

Does his praying involve asking?

'It does, but that's not its most important side. It's much more about engagement with God's presence. It's at that level that it's most important to me and I recognize that I very often fail in my prayer, but I still feel it's important to do it regularly.'

While talking about prayer, the rabbi went back to the importance of study. His booklet made it clear that such study 'is essential to all serious and sustained Jewish living'.[15] He said that, for him, the study of Torah was more analogous to reading poetry than to an academic discipline.

'Reading poetry is an endeavour to allow the vitality, spirit, sense of beauty, vision that the poet has had to come off the page and enter one, and that's something of what studying Jewish texts should be.'

The booklet stated, 'We hope, pray and are committed to working for a relationship of peace and understanding between Israel and other nations and between Judaism and other faiths.'[16] My question about truth and other religions he declared a complex one.

'I don't believe Judaism represents "The Truth" in a totally exclusive manner, in such a way that we are compelled to feel that people following other paths are wrong. This is not something I believe at all. I believe it is deeply true, in the sense that it is founded on sincere, honest, profound and significant insights, which have been cultivated at the dedication of countless lives for thousands of years, and it's a great privilege to belong to it. At the same time I can respect and value other paths.'

Specifically about the relationship between Judaism and Christianity, the rabbi added that it had historically been 'very difficult', but he felt there had recently been movements in the right direction.

'Since Vatican II (particularly in the Catholic Church, but in others too) that difficulty has begun to be acknowledged, and that acknowledgment is extremely important.'

SOME REFLECTIONS

Let me again emphasize that the three people I interviewed for this section are not fully representative of the Judaism to be found in North London, let alone the rest of the world. I found it interesting, for instance, that, without prompting, all of them mentioned the Holocaust and none of them mentioned the modern State of Israel. I saw in them all a deep connectedness to history, a love of the rituals and culture and a sense of ongoing identity with and responsibility for a minority, and possibly threatened, community.

Although they spoke of different ways of thinking about and using the ancient texts of Judaism, there was a strong commitment to them as the basis for living in a good, worthwhile, ethical and satisfying way—what Jonathan Wittenberg described as 'a greater rhythm, an ancient, rich way of life'. This emphasis on living right can be contrasted with the Hindu emphasis on seeing right, and we may be able to find this divide continuing into the religions that come from these two ancient roots.

Probably also typical of Judaism is an awareness of the spiritual opportunities of the religion and of the possibility of a life beyond death, although none of the Jewish people I spoke to wanted to indicate that either held a central or essential place in the faith. The rabbi spoke of prayer and study as ways of 'finding God's presence', or of engaging with an immanent God, but didn't want to exaggerate its place in his life. Nicola spoke of having 'dipped in and out' of spirituality at different stages in her life, and Vernon said he didn't have any firm hopes beyond death, but added that this was probably his own fault for not working at it. He 'trusted' that God would be there and expected him to be much 'more understanding about certain human behaviour than other human beings'. Vernon Mark was the first person so far to talk about the need for forgiveness. This is a theme that will return.

As we might expect with a religion that has never sought converts and has often been on the receiving end of aggressive conversion tactics, none of them spoke about mission. I was interested also that Jonathan Wittenberg did not find any problem with believing that Judaism was 'deeply true' but not in a way that compelled him to say that people who followed other paths were wrong.

We are now going to move on to listen to people from the two great religions that split off from these two ancient ones— Buddhism and Christianity.

CHAPTER 8

LISTENING TO BUDDHISTS

London was on alert for terrorist activity in the run-up to Christmas, and the firemen were on strike, on the cold November afternoon when I set off into London to make contact with the Jamyang Buddhist community. As I walked through Waterloo station, a public announcement was made to evacuate the station, because of a reported emergency. I emerged with crowds of other anxious travellers into a dark, wet London screaming with sirens. Stopping from time to time to look at a road map, I set off through the back streets of Waterloo towards Kennington. Eventually I found the Old Court House in Renfrew Street, and stepped into an oasis of calm.

THE JAMYANG BUDDHIST CENTRE

Tibetan Buddhism is a visual, colourful tradition and, having been supplied with a cup of hot peppermint tea, I was shown around this most unusually and beautifully restored Victorian building. In the central shrine, bowls of water were being placed in front of a gleaming statue of the Buddha, standing in the position of what clearly had been the judges' bench in the Old Court. Above the doors were signs still cut into the stone, saying 'Solicitors' and 'Witnesses'. Pictures on the walls of the reception area showed His Holiness the Dalai Lama and the Spanish boy Lama Osel Rinpoche, who is recognized as the reincarnation of Lama Yeshe, the founder of Jamyang. The Centre has a resident Tibetan teacher, Geshe Tashi Tsering.

I ended up in the corner of another colourful room operating as a vegetarian café, to meet Estelle Rose and then Jonathan Underwood, both born into Jewish families, but converted into Buddhism in their adult lives.

ESTELLE ROSE

The move from Judaism to Buddhism seemed an interesting one to me. Estelle said:

'It's difficult why people choose a different religion from the one they were brought up in. I was born Jewish and obviously it's a mainly Christian culture. I married a Hindu and I worked in the Asian community in the East End for a long time, where most of the people were Muslim.'

So what had attracted her to Buddhism?

'This particular type of Buddhism concentrates on training your own mind so that you can be peaceful with whatever is going on around you. It's more like a philosophy because you don't have to believe in anything. You believe in other people, but you don't believe that anybody's in control of it all, holding it together, creating it. I just felt it fitted in with the way I wanted it to be.'

She found the Geshe was very clear in interpreting Buddhism for the way Western people think. Estelle told me she was a grandmother and a volunteer at the centre, helping with the carer's group programme.

'I was a lecturer in community education before, so I'm interested in the community work which they're just starting here. I think it's a new direction for Buddhism to become involved in community work, so it seemed to suit me very well. I can do just a day or two here and there, as my health hasn't been very good.'

Estelle was clear about what her new faith gave her.

'It gives you a direction; you've always got some sort of practice that you can do, which is about getting your ego out of the way, so that you can see things more clearly. Having a structure of meditation each day gives you strength and focus.'

Knowing that the Buddha taught that the goal was enlightenment (seeing things as they really are) and nibbana,[17] I asked her about the goal she was working towards:

'For me personally, I would just like to be able to understand a bit more—feel more useful, I suppose, more part of everything that was going on.'

I asked her if there was some goal for her beyond this life and she remarked that she felt it might take her quite a few lifetimes. So, I asked, what is the eventual goal?

'This type of Buddhism teaches that you don't die after enlightenment. You keep on being reborn in order to benefit all sentient beings until everybody is enlightened. All those previous Buddhas who've achieved enlightenment to help us are around, but they're sort of in a different dimension.'

I asked Estelle how important it was to her that other people should find out about and follow this way.

'I don't think it matters really, if what they're doing is making them happy—if they're finding strength from the faith they have, or even if they don't have any faith.'

Might she recommend it to someone who was unhappy?

'I don't think that I would, actually. I would want to be with them in a way that made them feel better. I get on with other people more, because of the calmness that my practice of Buddhism gives me, but I don't feel that people should change whatever it is that gives them strength. Since I started coming here, people have said, "Why do you want to do that?" but I didn't give an answer and now they don't ask me any more. I think they know that whatever I'm doing is making me feel focused.'

JONATHAN UNDERWOOD

Jonathan Underwood had been held up in his journey across London too, but joined me later in the café. He had been coming to the Jamyang centre for about three years, since a relative stranger gave him some leaflets about it. For some of that time, he had worked full-time as a manager for the centre. I enquired about his religious background and he said that his family was 'kind of Jewish'.

'When I started looking for a spiritual path, I went to the synagogue quite a few times. I don't know if I didn't try hard enough or if it wasn't appropriate for my mind at that time, but I felt no connection with Judaism. I came to Buddhism and immediately felt very comfortable and rooted here, and that's a strong feeling that's remained for a number of years.'

I asked him how his faith made his life better. He smiled.

'Yes, my Dad asked me this last Christmas. He said, "What does Buddhism do for you?" I couldn't answer him. It's hard to come up with a spontaneous answer every time, but what I frequently say is, it allows me to live in a way that feels meaningful and worthwhile. Finding something in which I can have faith gives me a sense of positivity and allows me to live in a way that feels good. Whether it is good objectively or not, I don't know, but it feels good.'

The main problem that he had experienced was meaninglessness, just lacking anything that felt worthwhile, just not finding anything satisfying.

'Having this sort of faith structure allows me to address that problem. The Buddhism I try to practise says the goal is to help other people—to become enlightened to benefit others. That's the formula we recite quite frequently; but realistically, in my heart, what I want to do is stop myself feeling pain. That's my real motivation. I aspire to be motivated by the desire to cultivate an altruistic mind that's more considerate of other people; but realistically, what I'm trying to do is to sort out my own problems, find answers, work with my own pain and find a way to get rid of it. That's the truth. It's not the party line.'

I was interested in how the Buddhist idea of rebirth fitted into his thinking about the goal.

'Whichever religious system you're dealing with, Catholicism, Buddhism or whatever, you come up against metaphysical ideas like original sin and soul, rebirth and karma. They're hard things to engage with, but I feel it makes sense to me that when something has started it will go on. I believe in cause and effect, so I think there will definitely be results, but what they'll be and whether I'll continue long enough to reach the ultimate goal, I don't know.'

Did Jonathan feel he could contact any sort of spiritual reality?

'We have these enlightened beings who are out there, working perfectly for the sake of others. Until you get to a certain level of understanding it's not possible for you to contact them directly, but I know I have contact with Geshe Tashi, the teacher here, and other Buddhist teachers too. They are very amazing people to be around. There is huge, unbelievable spiritual power that I didn't have a concept of until I experienced it.'

THE PLACE OF PRAYER

I asked Jonathan about the place that prayer and meditation, worship and ritual played in his life.

'It's called "doing your practice". The idea is that it's practice for the way that you act in the real world. You familiarize yourself with concepts like love or compassion, so that you employ them more in your daily life. It can be very motivating, thinking about the great qualities of the Buddha. You know there's something about praising things which is very inspiring, and there are prayers which motivate you, like "I will become enlightened for the benefit of all sentient beings." It's really an exercise, like going to the gym for your mind.'

So was it never a matter of making requests or asking for things?

'You could say that, but there's various ways of interpreting it. One way is to say when you go for refuge to the Buddha, Dhamma and Sangha,[18] the idea is that you're saying, "I will become the Buddha; I will realize the Dhamma; I will become a spiritual companion for my fellow practitioners." It has a sense of "No one else is going to sort it out; you have to do it for yourself."'

Jonathan then talked about the ritual of offering bowls of water that I had watched.

'Ritual works. For instance, there's a concept of offering in Buddhism. It's to do with generating generosity. There's a practice with bowls of water, [which feels like] a weird thing to do because you get water from the tap, so it's not exactly generous, but there's something about going through the process that is very grounding, and I've noticed that [after doing it], my mind is clearer and more relaxed than it was at the start. It works for me, anyway, but the idea in Buddhism is, if it doesn't work for you, just don't do it.'

I asked Jonathan if he wanted other people to become Buddhists too and he said:

'It's not like I'm saying that Buddhism is *the* way or the right way. It's *a* way and one that allows tolerance of other things. I would like there to be good knowledge of what Buddhism really is, so that this way would be available for everybody to choose, but I'm not sure it's suitable for everybody. The Buddha said several times that you shouldn't be attached to anything, including the Dhamma. The Dhamma is a raft to get you across the river.'

Then he told me a story about a Christian priest speaking at the cremation of Lama Yeshe.[19]

'The priest said he wanted to talk about the similarities and differences between Christianity and Buddhism. "At the start," he said, "there are many similarities. In the middle process there are a lot of differences and then at the end, there's a coming together." He explained that at the start of the journey there are similarities like the belief in love and compassion. In the middle part you have to relate to technical things like *samsara* and *nibbana*, soul and God. Then you come to the point of realization and that's the point of coming together. I think that the goal of all religions is the same.'

THE FRIENDS OF THE WESTERN BUDDHIST ORDER

Very much aware of the enormous variety in the ideas and practices of Buddhism, even in London, where there are probably more than 100 different groups, I contacted Vajrana, the Communications Office of the Western Buddhist Order, based at the London Buddhist Centre in Bethnal Green. People who have become members of this Order take on Buddhist names, and Vajrana arranged for me to meet Priyananda and Vagisvari at a new centre they were building in Holloway Road.

The builders were still working and we talked above the noise of hammering and drilling. The centre had quite a different feel to it from the Old Court House in Kennington—a set of modern offices and seminar rooms rather than an exotic place of worship.

PRIYANANDA

Priyananda, who comes originally from New Zealand, told me that he was ordained as a member of the Western Buddhist Order 24 years ago at the age of 23, after being raised as a Roman Catholic.

'Until my mid-teens I considered myself a Christian, but then I think I became disillusioned. It wasn't anything dramatic. I just didn't feel Christianity was for me. When I was about nineteen I really started looking around. I was particularly interested in methods of meditation and quite quickly came upon Buddhist meditation. I was very fortunate that in Auckland, New Zealand, there was a centre of the Western Buddhist Order. I quickly took to both Buddhism and the particular approach that is taken in the WBO. I think it just made sense to me. I found Sangharakshita's[20] exposition of Buddhism very compelling. He wasn't trying to cloak it in any sort of mysticism, but just tried to make it present-able and understandable. Buddhism made sense, but I was also attracted by the person because here was someone who was living, breathing his religion and I was really looking for this.'

Priyananda told me that Sangharakshita is a Londoner, but he spent 20 years in India as a monk.

'He's always taken a decidedly ecumenical approach. There isn't one school that is supreme or has the whole answer. He sees the whole canon, the whole teaching body, as meaningful for us. I was very much attracted to that approach. I wasn't looking for a culture. I was looking for an answer to the existential questions and I liked this idea of taking Buddhism from an Asian context and seeing that it's universal.'

Priyananda now finds himself a senior member of the Order. Since moving to England in 1991, he's been working for the Karuna Trust, which raises funds for social projects in India—mainly education for children and women—but he is moving on in January, hoping to do more teaching work and be more involved in the new centre.

When I asked him how his faith made his life better, Priyananda said that he found this question interesting because he had been thinking of writing something about his life.

'I think it's got to do with the area of meaning—actually having meaning in life. That was what I was looking for 24 years ago and it's something that was painful, a matter almost of life and death at that stage. So if there's a benefit, it's that sense that life has a meaning, which can be summed up as compassion.'

I asked him how the two aspects of Buddhism—compassion and detachment—could be held together. He thought it could be a productive existential question but he hadn't, in practice, found it a problem at all.

'It's as if there are two tendencies in human nature. One is to want to leave the world, but there is a contrary tendency, which is to go towards other human beings to help them. In practice it's not a problem. You go about being progressively less attached to things, but in a way you become more positively involved with people.'

'A sort of selfless compassion?' I asked.

'Yes, exactly that.'

THE GOAL

We moved on to the subject of the goal of his religious practice and he said again that this was something he'd been reflecting on.

'Traditionally it's defined as enlightenment—and moving toward that. It's normally spoken of as development of both wisdom and compassion, a sort of twinfold awakening, so it's got to do with seeing into the nature of things. It's not like switching on a light; this is why Buddhism talks of a path. I see it as progressively moving towards a deeper and deeper experience of the truth, of reality. Interestingly, I think I define it in terms of deepened friendships as much as deepening experience.'

Priyananda said that when he first became a Buddhist, he used to think that he was just going to have a meditative experience which would be awakening or enlightenment.

'This is valid, but it's only half the story. The other side is that one is in more profound connection with people, which is why we place quite a strong emphasis on friendship in our tradition. We don't like to think of enlightenment as being something I'll do next year or in ten years' time. I think of it as something that's happening now—that I'm waking up now.'

Was he thinking in terms of the process taking several lives?

'Personally, I'm not. I want to make the breakthroughs now and then be available to help other people in the world. If one can conceive of enlightenment at all, it's simply an ongoing process of selfless activity.'

When I asked if he felt there was some spiritual reality he could contact, he said that this too was a question that interested him, because there were so many people coming into Buddhism, as he did, from strongly Christian traditions.

'Is there a personal being in Buddhism, in the way Jesus Christ exists for Christians? I'd say yes, basically. There is quite profound philosophy here, but basically yes, there is a personal experience of the Buddha. One could get different answers from different Buddhists, but it is comparable with Catholicism where there is a very strong personal relationship. It actively helps me in my life. Where it departs from Christianity is that that being, that reality, is not a creator. You could say basically it's the Dhammakaya—the Buddha nature—that one contacts through one's practice. It's spoken of as beyond time, so in a sense it's always present. Strictly speaking, people say that when the Buddha died he was neither annihilated nor reborn, but I think through experience one can say the Buddha is always present and so is a spiritual reality that one can contact.'

PRAYER

Priyananda said he did pray but, having been raised in a prayer tradition by the nuns and brothers at his school, where every hour they used to do the rosary, praying for him is different now. Did he ask for help in his daily life?

'Well, funnily enough, I think sometimes I do. To say that prayer, in the theistic sense, and meditation are completely different is a mistake because actually there are times when I really need help and I pray in the way I used to do when I was seven years old. There is a spiritual reality—it can't get me out of a fix that I've created for myself—but perhaps it's that a perspective is provided, where I can see through the problem so that I can rise above it.'

He finished by saying that in relation to other religions, he just wanted people to have meaningful, happier lives.

'What I aspire to is positive dialogue without compromising on the truth, particularly between Christianity and Buddhism.

VAGISVARI

When I then met Vagisvari, she explained that she'd just become a mother for the first time at the age of 42. Before Reuben had arrived, she could set aside time to think, but as it was she'd just been out pushing him in the pram, looking at my questions and jotting down some thoughts as she walked. She said that following the pregnancy and delivery she wasn't sure that her brain had returned!

Vagisvari has been a member of the Western Buddhism Order for four years. She had been born and baptized into the Catholic tradition in Ireland, and the soft Irish accent was still very strong.

'My own experience of [Catholicism] was very narrow and restricting. It was completely full of dogma and regulations, shoulds and shouldn'ts. As an adolescent I found that very difficult because I was aware, always, of a strong sensitivity toward something else out there. I had a very strong intuition that there was something much more to life than just "this".'

Did her Christian tradition give her any way of exploring this intuition?

'Unfortunately it didn't. My own questioning and seeking was seen as a disruptive force and I was admonished that I didn't have enough faith, so every query was met with a static, fossilized kind of response. I felt very cramped and decided at 16 that this really wasn't the spiritual path for me, so my heart left it, as it were. When I came to London in my early 20s I began to go to philosophy classes. I'd tried a little bit of the hedonistic route, but I found that equally empty. My brother died when I was 20 and of course that was a huge, shattering experience. It makes you wonder, what on earth are we here for? Where's he gone? Why this and why that?'

Her journey into Buddhism began when the philosophy class looked at the Dhammapada.[21]

'It was my first ever introduction to anything Buddhist and I thought it was one of the most beautiful pieces of writing I had ever listened to. There was something about the truth embodied in those words, that poetry, that I felt I could resonate with. I thought, "That's it! That's the way it is." It was a very strong experience. So I found myself at the London Buddhist centre trying to find out what Buddhism was all about.'

A PERSONAL, PRACTICAL PATH

I asked her how Buddhism had made her life better.

'It's a very practical path and therefore it gives me loads of practices that I can tap into in order to carry on a process of transformation. It's something I have to do myself as an individual, and that's something I found quite different from my former religious experience. I really respond to that very positively because it's a way of being incredibly creative with your life. I feel that to be creative as opposed to being reactive all the time is very liberating and very freeing of the emotions. You feel you have a purpose in the world and don't have just to lie down, with the world rolling over you. That makes me feel already that I'm living a better life, an active life, not just like a robot getting bogged down in the same old patterns but appreciating that I don't have to be the way I always was. I can grow, develop and transform into a more truly human being.'

She described the problems of living a human life as 'dissatisfaction'.

'One could say suffering, but I don't necessarily mean all human beings suffer, but all human beings experience dissatisfaction. Something's not quite right in everybody's life, I think, and Buddhism addresses this very directly. If someone wants to find out why things are so dissatisfying, Buddhism has a way of helping them understand why that is the case and what the individual can do to cope with it.

'Buddhism makes it very clear that we don't see things the way they really are. Our mind is full of distraction. We shuttle backwards and forwards between relatively negative emotional states, greed, ill will, hatred and irritation. We think we know how the world operates, but we don't, and this causes a great deal of suffering, because we're pushing and pulling in the wrong direction all the time. People also feel very bogged down in the sense that they feel they can't change anything in the world out there. Buddhism can show you very directly that you have got an enormous amount of potential to change your mind, and therefore [to change] the way you see things and the way the world seems to you. Buddhism can help you, through practices, to be more comfortable in the world, to feel more responsible for the world and to really feel the excitement that comes from being able to change your own mind.'

SPIRITUAL INSIGHT AS THE GOAL

The goal of Vagisvari's religious life was 'spiritual insight'.

'Being able to see things the way they truly are, being able to perceive directly and experience the spiritual truth behind all of existence—that's my goal. It's very hard work putting it into practice. It would be incredibly naive of me to sit here and say, "Oh yes, I'll get there." You have to take the path step by step.'

I asked her if she was thinking in terms of reaching this goal in a future life.

'I don't, from a rational point of view, bother to think about it like that. I know there's plenty of material in the scriptures about several lives, but I'd really like to do it in one lifetime, because this is the life I am living now. This is my chance. it would be a terrible shame to waste it. Anything beyond this life is mere speculation.'

PRAJNAPARAMITA

When I asked Vagisvari if she felt there was a spiritual force or beings that she could contact in a personal way, there was a long pause. She was, she said, trying to understand the question, so, taking my cue from Priyananda, I made a comparison with Christianity and she came up with an answer rather different from his.

'That's a very interesting question. Aspects of the enlightenment experience have been revealed, or explained, in imaginative forms, so the iconography in Buddhism represents qualities like compassion, fearlessness, skilful action. Because Buddhism appeals not just to the rational mind but also to the imaginative faculty, we can relate through myth and symbol to the truth of Buddhism. So you can either approach it in conceptual, actual form or in myth and symbol, or indeed either at different times.'

'One aspect of the enlightened mind that I particularly relate to is a figure called Prajnaparamita. She's a figure who represents the perfection of wisdom. She's a woman of mature years, incredibly beautiful, incredibly self-contained. I've come into Buddhism through a quest for wisdom, so I have a special link with that figure. Now whether that figure exists in reality, or is an aspect of my own mind which resonates with the mind of the transcendental, I don't really know, but one way or another she represents to me the goals of the spiritual life and I have a personal connection with her because I meditate on her every day.'

When we started talking about how these truths had come to her, Vagisvari spoke of the Dhamma, and I asked her where it originated.

'The Dhamma is always there. [It] is that ultimate reality supporting every single thing. The Dhamma represents the ethical universe—just the way things are. We can live in resonance with that or we can live at odds with it, and it's my belief that when we do that we suffer. When we live more in accordance with that truth, then things begin to change and can continue to change radically until we are at one with that truth. As I understand it, Siddhartha Gotama[22] accessed this universal truth through his own efforts, and because he was such a good teacher and had 40 years to do it, he was able to communicate some of that experience. The disciples around him began to practise and could realize the same truth, and then down through the ages people were able to tap into Buddhism.

Was this truth for everyone?

'I would hope that every human being would be able to find the truth about life, for sure. I feel that for me the Dhamma represents the truth. I have no doubt about that at all, but I couldn't expect that everybody else would think or feel the same way. There are many other paths, and people should be free to choose whatever path they want. I do believe that; however, I think it's important to make the Dhamma available in the world, as a choice for people. That's why we're converting this old office block into a Buddhist centre, so that people can come in off the street if they want to find out about Buddhism. Buddhism is a personal invitation. It's impossible to conceive of any kind of coercion or telling people that this is what they should be doing.'

We had finished my questions but I asked her if she wanted to say anything else. Again there was a pause, then Vagisvari said:

'Yes. I'd like to say to everybody, if you are engaging in spiritual practices and it's clear to you that they are helping you go beyond yourself, grow and develop beyond your narrow habitual way of being, opening up new horizons and new vistas for you, then that's fine.'

And if they're not?

'Then please don't judge other people by your own restricted mind. Truly be honest with yourself. If what you are doing is confirming to you that everything is all right for you and everyone else is wrong, then change your mind.'

✢

MEETING A SRI LANKAN THERAVADA BUDDHIST

I had spoken to four Buddhists and got some fascinating answers to my questions but still felt that this section was not complete. I'd met four people converted in their adult life, two from Judaism and two from Catholic Christianity. Two had found their home in a Mahayana tradition and two in a modern, Western combination of Mahayana and Theravada Buddhism. So I contacted an old acquaintance, the husband of a former student of mine. Anil Goonewardene was born in Sri Lanka into a family that had been Buddhist for generations. He was brought up in the Theravada tradition practised there, and trained as an attorney and barrister. Since coming to England he has been actively engaged in teaching and writing about Buddhism and representing the Buddhist community, particularly in the field of education. He is involved in the Buddhist Society, the London Buddhist Vihara and the Amaravati Buddhist Monastery.

ANIL GOONEWARDENE

I sent Anil a copy of my questions and he wrote back with written answers, suggesting that we met to discuss them. I walked through the snow to meet

Anil at his home in West Finchley. I asked him first about the many different forms of Buddhism that people come across in the West today and he told me with the hint of a sigh:

'I spend half my life telling people that the current teaching all comes from the teaching of the one Gotama Buddha. The Buddhas of the past taught the same and the Buddhas of the future will do the same. This teaching—the Dhamma—is a part of nature. It's just how the world is. It's because it has developed in different cultural backgrounds that there are these peripheral differences, these different traditions.'

I told him where I had been and he said:

'Yes, and you can find Tai, Chinese and Japanese establishments in London and then there are the Nichirens, but it's not more diverse than any other religion.'

For an answer to my question about how his faith made his life better, Anil had written:

'The Five Precepts guide a person to live in harmony with themself, with the society and within the law.'

THE FIVE PRECEPTS

I asked Anil to explain what the Five Precepts are, and he told me:

'The first is translated as not to kill people, but that's a very narrow translation: it really means not to harm living beings. The second is not to take what is not given to you, or not one's due. The third is often translated not to indulge in sexual matters which are not proper, but a better word is "sensual" because it applies to all the senses. The fourth is not to indulge in wrong speech, and the fifth, not to take intoxicating drink, drugs, anything like that, because it interferes with the proper working of the mind.'

Anil wanted to say, however, that Buddhism is more than just an ethical system or a philosophy.

'I say it is a religion. I refer people to the Oxford English Dictionary where the meanings of the word "religion" are given.' It comes within those meanings.

He had written that the Noble Eightfold Path sets out the practice of Buddhism. Some traditions, he told me, explain this teaching as being the development of compassion and wisdom. It is this practice that makes Buddhism into a religion and points the way to coping with the problems and difficulties that confront people.

'When linguists translate the Pali word *dukkha*, and they have to use one English word, they use the word "suffering". I spend a lot of time trying to explain that that is a misrepresentation. *Dukkha* means mental non-ease, imperfection or unsatisfactoriness, but that's not a very elegant word.'

As an example he talked about the problem of finding meaning in life.

'Buddhism answers that the aim of life is to attain Enlightenment. The meaning of life is to make an effort to attain Enlightenment. Buddhism says there are three fires in a person—hatred, greed and ignorance. So ignorance is one of the difficulties, but it's not an insurmountable problem. It's just a matter of understanding how things are. Greed—here again some of the translations into English from the Buddhist text have been done by linguists, not by Buddhists, so they have used words which are not really accurate. It's not greed so much as attachment or wanting things.'

Thinking about what I had already heard, I asked him if it was largely a matter of coping with these difficulties at the level of your own mind, rather than changing the external world.

'It is mainly. Relating to the external world, there are certain things we can change, certain things we can't. For instance, in the winter there is snow and ice and we can't change that. So the mind has to adjust itself to accepting that, and if it does, then there is no stress. There is no "suffering", although having the snow is not perfect.'

NON-ATTACHMENT

I was interested in pursuing the idea of detachment, but Anil said he would rather talk about non-attachment.

'Attachment is something that creates these mental difficulties, so non-attachment is important. But not necessarily detachment because one has to live in the community and one has to work in harmony with the community There are six senses. These are like windows and the messages that come through them can create attachment. Some things are pleasurable, like music, but a person can get hooked on music, so it's that sort of attachment that people have to avoid, because attachment interferes with the proper balanced working of the mind. People need to have compassion, firstly for themselves and for others, but that's not an attachment. That's why Buddhism talks of "loving kindness", because the English word "loving" implies some sort of attachment and "loving kindness" doesn't.'

ENLIGHTENMENT AS THE GOAL

Anil wrote that the goal of his religious life was the realization of Enlightenment, nibbana and absolute reality.

'When the goal is reached, it's simply a state of consciousness. Someone realizes all the Buddhist teaching and then they realize that there is no self and, although they continue to live in harmony with the rest of the world, they are not at odds with anything and they are not trying to prove anything. The Buddhist teaching is that there is no soul or self—no enduring identity. Someone reaches Enlightenment because they have got free of attachment, ignorance and hatred, which is the glue which holds the strands of life together, [and so] these strands don't continue into another life.'

When I enquired how confident he was that he would reach this goal, Anil had written, '100%'.

'Gotama Buddha asked his followers to try out his teaching and test it for themselves. I am doing this step by step. The truth of all aspects of the Buddhist teaching can be verified by Buddhist practice.'

To the question of whether he felt that in any sense he made contact with, or could get to know, the spiritual reality that lies behind human existence, he had written:

'I am in contact with this reality all the time and am increasing my knowledge of it day by day.'

He was, however, unhappy with the word 'spiritual' because it had a specific meaning in Christianity. The 'reality' that he was talking about was the Dhamma, *the teachings, although he did also believe that there are heavenly beings, or deities, born on a higher plane. I asked him if they were available to help.*

'Yes, this is common to all the traditions of Buddhism. They are not *there* to help but people can ask them for some help. It might be that they can give them strength of mind or something like that. Although in the Japanese Pure Land sect they do say that once you are born in Amida's world he will lead you to heaven, that only means he can show the way. The realization for each person has to be by his own effort.'

Anil explained that according to the Theravada, Gotama Buddha is dead. The Mahayana, however, divide the Buddha into three, including an eternal Buddha-nature. He said:

'That idea is not found in Theravada, but it's not in conflict with anything the Theravada teaches.'

WORSHIP

This is why, for him, worship is not of the Buddha, because he is dead and gone.

'Worship is a form of meditation on the teaching. In this meditation I suppose people can communicate with certain heavenly beings, but Gotama himself is not there any more. People go to the temple and offer flowers or incense; they light lights. It looks like a ritual, as if they've got nothing else to do, but it has a meaning. For instance, when they offer the flowers to the image, it is to show that the flowers look nice now but in a couple of days they will have dried out, like the human body [does] in a few years. It shows the impermanence of everything.'

Anil had written, 'Through personal practice and understanding I am certain that the Buddhist religion leads to the truth.' When I met him he added:

'Buddhism has never been a proselytizing religion and has never been in conflict with other religions. People who follow other religions may be approaching the truth in their own way. If they wish to know about Buddhism we are happy to help them.'

He thought the Christians' idea that their religion was the only way was connected with European empire-building and colonialism. 'And you think it's time they grew out of it,' I commented. He gave a little smile.

SOME REFLECTIONS

Something that came across strongly to me in these conversations is the idea of the goal of religious life being spiritual insight—taking control of and transforming your own mind so that you can see the world differently and so be able to cope with and eventually escape from it. Estelle perhaps put it most simply: 'Getting your ego out of the way, so that you can see things more clearly.' I hope you could sense Vagisvara's excitement about discovering that people had the potential to change their minds and therefore the way the world appeared to them.

There is no creator here, no law-giver, no saviour, but this did not mean, for all of these Buddhists, that there was no one there to help. This transformation of the mind that they were seeking was, however, for all of them, something no one else can do for you. Jonathan said, 'No one else is going to sort it out; you have to do it for yourself', Anil that 'the realization for each person has to be by their own effort'. We will see quite a contrast to this in the next section, when I speak to some Christians.

In Buddhism you have to do it *by* yourself but not *for* yourself. I was surprised by the emphasis on compassion and friendship, on a selfless living for others, that came through these conversations, although some were, in the short term, more concerned with how their own lives felt now, with the need to eliminate the pains, the dissatisfactions, of life.

I was interested in the feelings that had driven the four converts towards Buddhism. Jonathan was 'just lacking anything that felt worthwhile' or 'satisfying'. Priyananda was 'looking for an answer to the existential questions' and an answer to a sense of meaninglessness that 'was painful, a matter almost of life and death'.

Vagisvara said she thought there was a sense that 'something's not quite right in everybody's life'.

The idea of prayer and ritual as imaginative, self-motivating exercises interested me, too. Jonathan thought the beginning and end of religions are the same; it's just the technical bits in the middle that are distinctive. As we move on to Christianity, you can decide for yourself if this idea is a plausible one.

CHAPTER 9

LISTENING TO CHRISTIANS

This book is addressed to Christians, to encourage them to think about their attitude to people of other faiths. I wanted, however, to include some conversations with Christians for several reasons—firstly because there are so many kinds of Christians, just as there are so many kinds of Hindus, Muslims and Jews. Listening to each other can be as important as listening to others. I hope it will be clear to readers that the three people I have interviewed in this section don't even begin to encompass the diversity within Christianity. As you read their comments, you may feel that the things these people say are not anything like the sort of answers you would have given to these questions. I hope this will bring home the fact that the same is true of the other religions we have covered—that the people speaking in every chapter of this book represent only themselves. None of these interviews can be used to draw conclusions about 'what Buddhists believe' or 'how it feels to be a Sikh'. They can show only a bit of how it feels to these particular people.

When some Christians say that their religion is unique in its apprehension of the truth, or its power to save, what they often mean is that their particular interpretation of the Christian story, the particular tradition in which they have been born or nurtured, is unique in this way, and that Christians who interpret the story differently can be as wrong as people who build their faith on a different story altogether. This way of looking at matters of faith makes quite a difference to the sort of broad comparisons some people make between religions.

I spoke first to Zoe Flatt, who had recently married Rick and moved from Finchley to a new job as youth worker at Brigadier Free Evangelical Church in Enfield.

ZOE FLATT

Zoe is a paid part-time youth worker but she told me that for her it was not a career, it was a calling.

'I'm a youth worker 24/7 and I would probably be if I wasn't paid for it, because it's what God's called me to and something I'm really passionate about.'

She runs a group for 'non-church kids' aged 10 to 14, where the leaders 'play mad games with them and give them the gospel'. She also oversees the teaching for all the young people in the church and runs an outreach, café-style drop-in.

'We have some "scallys" coming along to that. It's probably the most challenging work, but also the most rewarding.'

How she came to be there, Zoe described as an 'up-and-down roller-coaster ride'.

A BILLY GRAHAM MEETING

When Zoe was about 14 she went to a meeting at her church which was a live link-up from the Billy Graham mission taking place at Wembley. She was moved by what Billy Graham said about Jesus dying on the cross for her.

'I knew it all, but this was making it real for me, personally. I think God was saying, "It's time you took your faith on for yourself." They called people up to the front to make a commitment and my heart was pounding. I said to my friend, "Do you want to come with me?" and she was like, "Yeah, I do", so we both went off to the front with this overwhelming sense of love and excitement.'

Zoe's faith became more real to her when she was about 18.

'I went up to meet my brother in Scotland. He goes to a charismatic church, really "swinging from the chandeliers", and I was sitting in a prayer meeting, at the back, and they started praying and people started shaking and doing freaky things and I sat there thinking, "My God, what is going on?" I had my head down because I didn't want any of this coming to me. I said to God, "If this is real, then show me that you're here." I felt my legs shaking. It was very strange and then I felt this overwhelming peace, a really nice feeling; you just can't describe it.'

It wasn't until she was in her third year at university, however, that she decided she was 'really going to go for it'.

'I felt like a hypocrite because what I was saying I believed was not what I was showing. I think living the life of a Christian is the most important thing. I had to deal with an awful lot from my past, times when I'd messed up and not asked for God's forgiveness, so I did that. That was all very painful. Then God spoke to me about youth work and I said there was no way I could do it. I really wanted to, but I'm so inadequate, I've made mistakes in my life. So I prayed about it and it all happened really quickly. I just fell into it. I wanted to be a prima ballerina when I was little.'

I asked Zoe how her faith made her life better.

'I don't know that my life is better. In a worldly sense of "better" I'd probably say no, because if I wasn't a Christian I'd probably have a much better job and have my own house (I'm not complaining, I'm really blessed) and wouldn't have to be giving up my evenings and weekends—and then I think, no, because I wouldn't have God in my life and to me that would be a massive void. He's comforter, friend, someone who I can talk to. I've tried to invite him into every aspect of my life because I've found that when I do, even if things are really bad, it just seems better, because I'm not on my own. God's in there and he knows what he's doing and if I make a mistake he can turn that around for his glory.'

A HOPE IN HEAVEN

'I don't know how people manage without Jesus (I know that sounds really cheesy) but I don't know what you'd live for, because for me I've got a hope in heaven. That's a promise, because when I became a Christian that was my inheritance, and the amazing thing is that it's not about what I do, it's about what God's done and even if I mess up, I can still get to heaven because I can be forgiven. I find that totally blows my mind.'

The aim of Zoe's life was to share her faith with as many people as she could.

'I'm not ramming it down people's throats, but telling people what I believe and why I believe it, so that they can share in it as well—telling people who don't have a clue, that there's a major gift that God's waiting to give them. I'm called to go out and make disciples and tell as many people as I can about Jesus. I believe God's got a plan for each of our lives and I want to be doing what God has planned for me to do and receiving what God has planned for me to receive, and ultimately to be with him in heaven.'

How confident was she of achieving that goal?

'I'm very confident, because I believe when I became a Christian that was my ticket to heaven. When you become a Christian you receive the Holy Spirit: that is your deposit, guaranteeing your inheritance, and that eternal life starts now.'

I asked how she knew about these things and she told me it was because she had experienced God in her life.

'[I know it] because I've got a relationship going with him. I spend time listening to God. I can hear him speaking to me. Because I've experienced God and God is in me, I know that he's real. There's no doubt in my mind—today. Sometimes God is silent, but he knows what he's doing, which is good because I don't. Other people's experiences help too—listening to people talking about their experiences.'

'Was it just from experiences?' I asked her.

'No, it has to be grounded in what the Bible says. I've talked about God speaking to me, but if I thought God was speaking to me and it wasn't consistent with the Bible, then it would be because I'd been eating too much pizza! What God's written in his word stands true for ever and ever. You always have to go back to that.'

PRAYER AND WORSHIP

'Prayer and worship are fundamental things for me, a way of getting closer to my God, a way of connecting, and for me worshipping is a way of saying, "God, you're absolutely amazing." It's important to do it on your own, but coming together as "the body [of Christ]" is really important too. I try to pray every day and for me it's not just sitting down or getting on my knees, it's all day every day; it's just like talking to your friend, and I do pray for people and I've seen God answer those prayers. That's totally cool. I love it.'

I asked Zoe what part ritual played in her life and reminded her of Holy Communion.

'Yes, obviously, because it's a way of remembering what Jesus did when he died on the cross and the implication of that for me, and [it's about] sharing fellowship with other people.'

My last question was about how certain she was that what she believed was the truth and how important it was to her that other people believed it too.

'I'm certain this is the truth because Jesus said, "I am the way, the truth and the life", and that we come to know God through him. I can't see that there's any other way. The reason I believe that other people should believe it too is because I don't want people to go to hell and that is the alternative.'

I asked Zoe what she thought that meant.

'Being without God. I don't know what that means physically. Jesus talks clearly about heaven and hell and I think it's a reality, but I don't know what it means. It sounds really harsh and I think people get mixed up because they think God is sending people to hell, but God doesn't want anyone to go hell. God loves everybody and wants them all to be with him, but he's not making us like holy robots; he's giving us that choice. Even I choose to go against God a lot of the time, and the consequences of that show. You can see the collective consequences of our sins by switching on the news.'

She ended by saying:

'We should be making the most of every opportunity we have to tell people about Jesus. I know I don't always do it and it scares me that there are people who don't have a clue and people who have heard and say, "So what!" As Christians we are called to tell people about Jesus, because it's good news.'

BROTHER ANGELO

The second Christian I spoke to was a Franciscan friar. Brother Angelo had warned me that 'The Friary' was just an ordinary suburban house in a side street of Willesden. In fact, he told me, the house had been offered to the small band of brothers by the local parish church simply because it was too big for a curate.

Brother Angelo opened the door wearing a brown robe (habit) and sandals, and welcomed me into a small, simply furnished living-room. He explained that the brothers are Anglican Franciscans, a group that came into being during the 1920s but is related to the ancient Order started by St Francis of Assisi in the 13th century. Angelo is ordained as a priest in the Church of England, but the Franciscans are primarily a lay order.

'It's very unusual to be attached to a parish as we are here. The parish offered us the house simply to be a Franciscan "presence"; then inevitably we got drawn into helping with services, parish visiting and so on. Our life, like that of all religious, is based around the day of four Offices in chapel, plus a Eucharist.'

The brothers take vows of poverty, chastity and obedience, but Angelo explained that it's not a slavish, blind obedience.

'It is the obedience that comes from a common mind rather than an imposed discipline.'

I asked him about his own spiritual journey.

'I've always been a practising Christian. I had the usual sort of hesitations during adolescent years, but then I was becoming quite successful in business and I'd moved here to London and I developed psittacosis. I was really quite ill and in hospital for a very long time and came out partially paralysed, with no functional vocal chords. When something like that happens to you, all the things you've paid lip-service to are called into question. I went to live in a little house overlooking the river near Teignmouth in Devon, where I met a rather super priest who helped me through some of the questions—'Why did this happen to me? What have I done?'—all that sort of thing, which is a little immature but they have to be worked through. It was in the working through of that that some of the excess baggage of religion fell off and my prayer became very real.'

WHO AM I?

'God became very real because you can't be angry with someone you don't think exists. I was quite angry with God at the time, and that time of questioning gave me a different view of God and my relationship to God and what life was about, because in the middle of it all came that resounding question, 'Who am I?'— which is, I suppose, the question that haunts all of us. I believe now that you can only find yourself in relation to other people and in relation to God, however one may visualize God.'

Brother Angelo thought that one of the major problems of human life was finding a goal, knowing where you are going.

'I feel that as Christians we come from God—you can imagine a kind of elliptical orbit. We come from God; we touch the earth for whatever length of time our humanity lasts: we die, and we return "from whence we came". That gives completeness to my whole life. I think, "OK then, in this bit I have a particular responsibility to make right choices and decisions", and I can't make those choices and decisions except in relation to other people and in relation to what I think would be God's will for me.

'I believe that it is the will of God that every human person develop to the fullness of their… "potential" is not quite the right word, but it's the only one I can put here. Jesus gives us an example of what humanity can be. When people say, "Why are you a Christian?" the answer is, "Because Christianity has got Jesus Christ and the others haven't." Here is a model, someone I can look to, and I believe we need that as human beings.'

I asked Brother Angelo where prayer fitted into his life and he said that for him it was the expression of a relationship,

'This is why, four times a day, we centre ourselves back on what is the focus of our lives—our Lord Jesus Christ, and our relationship in him with God.'

A GOAL

'I think that the goal of my religion is to help me become uniquely me, and for me to help others become uniquely themselves. You can only do that, oddly enough, by sharing a great deal. There is a very real difference between the true development of oneself and being selfish, and so my religion helps me to get rid of the selfish element in order that, with others, we can together achieve that uniqueness which each one of us has.'

How confident was he that he would reach this goal?

'Well, I don't think I will in this life. For me there is the potential to become another Jesus, but when you look at the sort of man he was, even putting aside the miracles and so on, just look at the man! Oh dear, we're nowhere near arriving at that level, but we're all helping each other to do it.'

CHOOSING THE WAY OF SUFFERING?

Prompted by some thoughts I had had after talking with the Buddhists, I asked him if he thought following Jesus involved choosing the way of suffering, and he replied that he didn't think it was actually that.

'To read the Gospels is to recognize that when we say Jesus was the perfect man, it was partly because Jesus had perfect insight. I think he knew from the moment he started his ministry that he was going to be so much against the traditional teachings of the day and (like the ancient prophets before him) so critical of what others were very satisfied with that it was going to end up in bother. In a sense, then, we can say that he chose that path, [but] I think, for the average Christian, you don't talk about choosing the way of suffering so much as recognizing that suffering is a part of our humanity. Suffering comes in a variety of ways and usually it's been caused by other human beings, either inadvertently or deliberately, and that's part of our being members of the human race. I think one of the difficulties of our modern day is that everyone is looking for something to take away the pain—"Give me something to stop the suffering!"—and it can be anything from deep psychoanalysis to Valium, as though life must be absolutely devoid of any suffering. I think that's impossible unless you are prepared to say that there musn't be any love or care or concern for one another either.'

When I introduced the subject of 'the truth', he said:

'In a sense the truth is the truth; I don't think the truth changes, but our perception of it does, dependent on where we are at any given moment. There was a moment when I felt, "This is what brings it all together; this is what makes sense of my being here, of the universe somehow or other", and the fact is that we name that key point which makes it all make sense "God".'

THE TRUTH THAT WE ARE VALUABLE

'The truth, in the end, is our heavenly Father and that sense of belonging, of being created for a purpose, of being valuable. Today we hear such a lot about people who have so little self-esteem or people who are undervalued. I remember the day I went home to my mother from Sunday school and said, "I've just discovered there is no one else on this earth like me", and I remember my mother saying, "Well, thank God for that!" It was a little glimmer of truth. The second thing—I believe with every atom of my being that if I had been the only person in existence on that hill that day, Jesus would still have been crucified for me, and that is my value and I bring that unique value to every situation. Nobody can replace me and therefore I must esteem myself and develop the right kind of self-respect, which is quite the opposite of arrogance.'

Brother Angelo thought that certainty could easily come across as arrogance.

'[This is what happens] sometimes, with fundamentalists of any faith, who are so convinced that they are right. We can be right at a particular point in the way, when we interpret that view of truth at that time, in that situation, but then a little later, through experience, through prayer, through the different situations in which God has placed us, discover that [although] truth doesn't change, my perception of it is different from [my] earlier view.'

THE CHURCH'S MISSION

I asked Brother Angelo how important he thought it was that other people should share his view of the truth.

'I think because our Lord said, "Go and make disciples of all nations", we all have this mission. It's part of the Church, and as long as I am part of the Church I must have that mission. I think our responsibility is not to bludgeon people into accepting the faith, although one prays they will. The ideal is to share what you have already discovered. I think there's a real danger in applying fundamentalist translations to words that Jesus uses, and therefore you wouldn't hear me quoting very often, "No one comes to the Father but through me." That's too often taken to mean that unless you're a Christian you're doomed to eternal hellfire or something, and I don't think that's what Jesus meant. I think he meant, "Because of what I've done, because of who I am, I've opened the way for you to come."

'You have, not only by what you teach but by who you are and how you live, to share at a level at which people can make their own choice, because, when you think about it, that's what Jesus did. For most people Jesus was just among them, sharing their problems, "being there for them". I think that's a marvellous phrase because sometimes that's all we can do. The words don't come; you can't turn the clock back; you can't perform a miracle, but you can be there. It's not my job to go round frantically trying to save people. Jesus has done that—that's a fact; they have to make it their own by their response to it, and all we do is create the space in which the Holy Spirit of God can work.'

MANY PATHS TO GOD?

'I read in a book the other day that there are as many paths to God as there are people to follow the paths. Now that would make it very easy to sweep everything aside and say, "Well we're all the same, aren't we?" [But] we're not; the way in which we make the response is very different. We're not all the same, and sometimes I think what has been missing from the ecumenical movement is the pain of division, because if you think "We're all the same", you never make efforts to understand, or to recognize the differences, to respect each other in those differences. When you feel pain about the divisions between you, then you really want to go out and do something about unity, about understanding, sharing and respect. One of the miracles of humanity is the wonderful variety and difference, but if we allow the differences to make chasms and great emptinesses between us, then we're never going to be truly human.'

✝

There is a sizable Greek and Turkish community in North London, largely originating from Cyprus. While the Turkish Cypriots are most likely to be Muslim, the Greek Cypriots are most likely to be Christians from the Eastern Orthodox tradition. I decided it would be interesting to do my last interview for this section with a member of a Greek Orthodox church. I approached the priest at a church I knew of and was transferred up to the Archbishop and down again until a name was suggested. Tom Kasapi is a young accountant, born in London. He spent some of his early years in Cyprus but returned with his family to Britain when they lost their home in the war with Turkey.

TOM KASAPI

Tom Kasapi is a member of a Greek Orthodox church in Highbury, where he is the treasurer and does 'whatever is needed'. This can include taking part in the procession of 'the holy gifts' during the service or, as on one occasion, being up until midnight cleaning the floor.

I asked Tom about his own spiritual journey and he told me that at about 13 or 14 he decided he wanted to know more about his faith.

'I didn't understand it. The service was all Greek to me! The problem is that we speak a dialect in Cyprus. The Greek we use in church is more classical, more poetical. I was at a service one Easter, and I saw an English monk [with] a service book in his hand, in ancient Greek. He was disabled and in a wheelchair. I started going to help him out and asked him questions and learnt about my faith from him. That's how it started. I'm now going once a month to Cambridge where they've started a study group, and I read a lot.'

I asked Tom how his faith made his life better.

'I think when you haven't got any faith... I'm an accountant— if I was just staring at numbers all day and totalling them up, [imagine] the pointlessness of it! If anything goes wrong, I've got faith there. I trust in God, so if I feel bad I might go and cense the house or say a prayer or go to church and light a candle, and it just makes things better. When you have faith you can say, "It's not important compared with eternity." So it puts things in perspective. It gives me a will to live, a reason to help others. It's a background to life.'

WHY ALL THIS SUFFERING?

I asked him about the problems of human life and he said:

'The fact that we die. The pointlessness of life. You see all that suffering and think, "If God exists, why is he allowing this?"'

His faith gave him answers.

'For one thing, suffering gets you closer to God, but secondly this life is only a drop in the ocean compared to your whole life. Death isn't the end of a life; it's a beginning. This puts everything into perspective.'

The goal of his religious life was 'to learn to repent'. This was not an answer I was expecting, so I asked him to explain.

'You ask for forgiveness and then, quite often, you go on to do the same thing again. To learn to repent properly, you've got to achieve something, you've got to move on. God forgives as long as you come with a contrite heart, but the aim is not to be trapped by the evil around you, by your temptations.'

I asked him if there was a goal beyond death that he was aiming at.

'Obviously I want to go to heaven, but it's not a goal in that I want to say that I'm entitled to a place in heaven. I don't think that any of us has ever got a right to it. I have to believe and trust in God, and it's a gift from him. I just trust about things like that basically. I don't like to look too far ahead in this life, let alone the next one.'

When I asked him if he felt that God was someone whom he could contact or get to know, he said:

'Yes of course. It's amazing how, in your life, you see things happen.'

He told me that when he first qualified, his brother's friend's wife's sister ('We're Greek!' he explained) heard of a job for him, and he said a prayer to the patron saint of accountants, and sent his CV off. Twice he lost faith but in the end the job was his.

'I didn't really have the experience for such a big firm, but every time I doubted, God showed me [that I could trust him]. You can see it in lots of things that you do.'

THE JESUS PRAYER

Tom felt that prayer, worship, ritual and meditation were all linked.

'I say the Jesus Prayer when I'm on the bus or tube or walking to work. I try to say it whenever I can.'

He explained that the prayer is 'Lord Jesus Christ, Son of God, have mercy on me, a sinner.' It is the basic prayer for meditation in the Orthodox tradition.

'The monks would say it a thousand times a day so that they became completely immersed in it. You can say the first phrase as you breathe in and the second as you breathe out, or you can do it with standing and prostrating, so that there is a rhythm to it.'

He had read a book in which a pilgrim is taught this prayer.

'He learns it and practises it until he realizes that each breath is a prayer. It had become involuntary. I've never attained this. I don't know that I ever will: I'm too easily distracted, but basically it's something I try to do.'

RITUAL

I asked Tom about ritual and he said that Greek Orthodox worship was very symbolic.

'You need to read a lot to understand some of the things we do. That's why I'm always reading.'

'Were the rituals helpful,' I asked him, 'even if people didn't understand all the symbolism?'

'I've studied a lot, so probably my religion is too much in my mind and not enough in my heart. I was raised in the West. I'm trained like that. Some of the older people don't seem to have all that knowledge. They haven't even read lots of the Bible; they just listen when it's read in church, [but] quite often you ask them something and they reply, and you think, "Oh, the wisdom there, the spirituality!" It's not the knowledge, it's more the practice; it's the living of the faith.'

Tom had studied maths and chemistry before doing accountancy, because he wanted to know how things worked, but he wasn't convinced that science had all the answers.

'Science didn't explain anything to me. Chemistry is based on postulates, assumptions. I think to myself, "This isn't science any more; it's faith. It's the religion of science."'

He now believes the Church has better explanations than science. He said that you could see the way that God had moved and inspired all the stages in the production of the Bible, but added that Orthodox Christians also used a lot of other writings, mainly from the Church Fathers.

'You need the Church to guide you—to help you understand the Bible. You don't get all that by reading it by yourself, but often people have too much pride in themselves. They think they can work it out. Pride is our biggest sin. You get these sects who break away. They read the Bible and think they understand it all. You need more than that.'

ICONS

Because it was a subject that interested me, I asked him about icons. He told me:

'An icon is not an idol. We don't worship them; we venerate them. Whether that's a technicality, I don't know. The first icon was Christ: he revealed God to us. Before that, they weren't ready to have any kind of pictures from heaven, because they didn't understand enough. Now every icon, whatever saint it is, is an icon of God, because the saints had God within them. The person painting it would pray and fast and he would bless the wood and the paints, but we don't believe God is specially in the icon. God is everywhere and he's in everything; the icon just focuses you. You are reminded of a saint's life; it makes you remember your faith.'

I asked Tom if he thought the Christians of the East see the relationship between spirit and matter in a different way from the Christians of the West and he agreed that they did.

'We believe we are both matter and spirit. We believe you need to use the material to reach the spiritual. That's why we fast. We think you need to use your body, like when you do prostrations, because God created the body as well. That's one of the reasons we don't have cremations, because we are an icon of God, we are a holy temple of Christ.'

THROWING THE BABY OUT WITH THE BATH WATER

Tom felt that when the Protestants rebelled against the rigid views within Catholicism (during the Reformation), they 'threw the baby out with the bath water'.

'They rebelled completely against it and threw everything out and have lost a lot because of that. It's good to see now that some Anglican churches have started putting a few icons back here and there. That's something.'

Someone had suggested to him that it all started from when the Catholics added the filioque *clause to the creed.*[23] *From then, he thought, things went wrong*

'If that's simplistic I don't know, but they seemed to separate the spiritual and the material. The West took the view that matter is dirty or sinful, whereas, as you can see in the New Testament, the body is resurrected as well. Jesus' resurrection body is both spiritual and material. We worship the spirit through the material and there's nothing wrong with that.'

IS THIS THE TRUTH?

I wanted to talk to Tom about his ideas of truth in religion, so I asked him, if he felt that this was the truth, did he believe it was the truth for everyone? He answered with a simple 'Yes'. 'And the other religions are wrong?' I asked.

'Yes, basically they are wrong. I mean, if I didn't believe that, I wouldn't believe my own religion. If people say there's one God and he manufactured himself differently in different cultures, that's not something I can accept. God is Christ—full stop. Whether he forgives people who are isolated and don't know about Christianity, I don't know. It says you're only saved through Christ, but I don't know. Who does? I can't answer for God on that.'

He thought Catholics and Protestants were wrong in their inter-pretations of matters of faith.

'They believe in Christ, which is something. I'm not saying they can't be saved, but when you don't believe that the bread and wine are the body and blood of Christ, to me that's insulting to God. You have to respect these things. It's respecting the material and the spiritual side at the same time.'

Perhaps because of the look on my face, Tom asked me if I was a Christian and I confessed to being a Protestant. He added:

'I would only say that if someone asked. I wouldn't want to push my beliefs on anyone else. We've all got the free will to choose the right from the wrong. Maybe he forgives. We can only trust in God and his love.'

SOME REFLECTIONS

In these interviews I had met three very different people, but each in their own way gave Christianity a central role in their thinking and living. Zoe, among the youngest of the people I interviewed, and Brother Angelo, among the oldest, were both currently working full-time for the Christian Church. Tom, with many of the other people I interviewed, shared the experience of being part of an immigrant community, but, unlike most of them, also shared in the majority religion of the people he was living among.

We have heard, and will continue to hear, a lot about God's mercy and grace—the possibility of receiving his forgiveness and the gift of salvation—but I found it interesting that all these three Christians talked about putting their hope in what God had done in Jesus. 'It's not about what I do,' Zoe said. 'It's about what God has done.' Brother Angelo interpreted Jesus' words about being the only way rather differently from Zoe, but said he thought Jesus was saying, 'Because of what I've done… I've opened the way for you.' Tom said that heaven was 'a gift from God… It's not something I could do anything to get.' Perhaps this explains a confidence we rarely see in the other Semitic religions.

Other things that caught my eye were the 'Jesus Prayer', which reflected the Hindu idea of filling your mind with thoughts of God, and the importance to all of them of growing in holiness, or as Zoe put it, 'living the life of a Christian' rather than just professing it.

Brother Angelo had been prompted to explore his faith by those existential questions we have heard others asking—'Why did this happen? Who am I?'—and had found answers not only in a personal faith but also in living with and for others.

I noted with interest Brother Angelo's idea that the wonderful variety and difference within humanity was something that we should embrace and celebrate rather than letting it make 'chasms and great emptiness between us', and his idea that what makes Christianity unique is that 'it's got Jesus Christ, and the others haven't'.

LISTENING TO MUSLIMS

The morning I went to visit our local mosque, there was a torrential downpour. The streets were flooded and when I arrived the cloak-room was piled high with dripping coats and scarves. A group of girls from one of the local secondary schools had walked over to the mosque to learn about Islam. They were sitting with wet hair on the carpet in a simple prayer room, asking questions of a Muslim woman. Some of the girls were wearing headscarves and they were asking about the way Muslim women dressed, about Ramadan, the month of fasting, and about how the times of prayer worked throughout the year.

Mufti Battula came down the stairs in a white tunic and hat and led me, shoes off, through another prayer room to his office, which was full of modern computer equipment. The mosque is a smart but modest conversion of a large house which stands next to a DIY store in North Finchley and opposite an Anglican church. Mufti Battula told me there were about four hundred Muslim families within a five-mile radius of the mosque and they came from all backgrounds, roughly a third from the Middle East, a third from Africa and the Caribbean and a third from 'the subcontinent'—India, Pakistan and Bangladesh. The mosque caters for them all by holding regular prayers.

MUFTI BATTULA

I asked the Mufti if all the worshippers at the mosque were Sunni Muslims.

'Out of 400 of the families, 345 are Sunni. I know about four or five are Shi'ah. There could be more, because they don't display their difference here.'

I asked him about his own religious background and he told me his father was a simple textile worker in India, who wanted all his children to become Muslim clergy.

'I have four brothers. Two couldn't cope with the religious schooling and ran away and became doctors. Those who remained were trained in a residential school. We studied Arabic, Persian and Urdu. I had always wanted to study English and modern sciences. When I had the chance I started learning English and then I had the idea to come here. It took me three years to learn English: then I did GCSE, A' level, a BSc and an MPhil.'

He felt now that, having been through both systems of education, he was the product of the best of both worlds.

'I've had a traditional religious, clerical background, from the medieval times, but then I've cross-bred my religious knowledge with modern knowledge. I represent modern Islam, with the combination of rationality, enlightenment and practicality, rather than being bogged down with medieval thinking and backwardness. I'm here as a liberal Muslim clergyman.'

The Mufti had been living in this area for about twelve years.

'When I came, because of my religious knowledge and my religious title, they put me in the mosque as a trustee. At the moment I'm the senior Imam as well. There are three or four Imams under me who have different functions. Some do daily prayers; some help with education sessions, some with other services. I earn my livelihood through computer work and household work, protecting my wife and children.'

That explained the computers. Mufti Battula had diverted a couple of phone calls already and he explained that he runs a national helpline.

'I have the authority to give a religious opinion, a written verdict of Muslim law. That gives me the title of "Mufti". It's like a court judgment. So I run a helpline across the country. People present me their social and religious problems and I give them advice and, if they need one, a court ruling in writing—an authentic Islamic legal opinion. Most of the time it's about marital discord, from men and women, family problems, and then of course smaller things, mainly nowadays financial issues like mortgages, bank loans, and work ethics. People are becoming more conscious of their work, of where they are working and for whom they are working.'

I asked him how his faith made his life better.

'I find solace and tranquillity in my belief in the unity of God, the unity of the universe and of mankind, and in the creator, who has given us life. I am at peace with God. I try to understand what the will of God is and try to interact with the whole of humanity as God would want me to. I want to make myself most useful, not just to the Muslim community, but all the neighbourhood. I am even interested in animal rights! I find harmony and peace in these beliefs and practices, following the commandments of God and trying to fulfil the will of God by serving the people.'

The Mufti thought that as far as day-to-day problems were concerned, most human beings managed very well.

'Management of these 70 years is not that much of a problem, but Islam takes the long-term view that this life is just a phase; death is not the end of life.'

AN EXPLANATION FROM ECONOMICS

Because he was an economist, he said he could explain it best in terms of disposable income.

'This life is a life to live and enjoy, and to be useful serving humanity, but we also see it as an investment opportunity, to get salvation and life eternal. By being good and useful to humanity, I make myself worthy of living an eternal life with God. Whatever income we get, if all we do is spend it we will suffer at the end, not having a pension, not having any savings; but if we save from our current income and put it in an income-rendering investment or pension scheme, then we are going to have comfort at the end when we need it most.'

I asked him what the goal of his religious life was.

'First of all, my goal is to be thankful to our God and try to please our Lord by acting in the manner he wants for us to live, by serving people, by making myself useful and by not creating any mischief. It's like our boss here is God and we want to do everything we can to please him, so to get the reward. This involves not just doing what is my duty, but going beyond the call of duty. The eventual goal is to be told by our God, "I'm pleased with you and your work", and the ultimate reward is to enter paradise.'

How certain was he of reaching this goal?

'We can never be certain because there's no means of me knowing, so what we do is live our life 50 per cent hope, 50 per cent fear. We believe in a day of judgment where there will be a final account presented, a balance sheet of whatever you did in your life—whether or not you are still in [the] red.'

GOD'S MERCY

I asked him how much in the end it would depend on God's mercy.

'It depends entirely on God's mercy, because we've been given life without our own asking or choice, so the life itself was granted by the sheer mercy of God. This is the chance for us to do good, but eventually it's by the mercy of God alone that we will be able to achieve any goal or objective. Of course justice is there. God would not be unjust to us. No, life is 100 per cent sheer mercy; our salvation is from sheer mercy. In between we are just trying our best.'

How had the truth of Islam come to him?

'Muhammad (peace and blessing be on him) was the person who first introduced it. He said, "I am appointed the messenger of God, and I am here to tell you what God wants from humanity." That knowledge, in the form of the holy book, and in the form of the *Traditions*,[24] has come to us through generation after generation. We hear the story and read the holy scripture and study it and contemplate it, and we see a billion people doing the same and finding peace and solace, and we know that this is the religion.'

To my question about whether he felt he could make contact with God or get to know him, he gave a confident 'Yes'.

'We are personally asked by God—it's like a five-times-a-day invitation—"Come to the appointment and try to offer the best thing you have for me." For God we just have some prayers and thankfulness; that's it, nothing else. In the formal prayer that we do here in the mosque, we think we are communicating with God and God is responding to us.'

He then raised the question of how you know that God has heard you.

'We know that God has responded when we see things come true. Many people ask me, "What is the proof that your prayer has been answered?" I say, I'll give you a small proof, convincing or not—the fact that you are still asking God. If your prayer had not been accepted, you would have turned away from God and found something else to do, but if you are still communicating with God, this means you are among the blessed ones, to keep in constant touch with him and be happy, whatever portion of your prayer has been granted.'

PRAYER

'Prayer is the essential organizer of our life. You heard what was being said to the schoolchildren: because of the continual moving of the time of our appointment with God, because it's decided by the times of sunset and sunrise, there is four hours of difference throughout the year. So we grow very conscious of time, very alert. It's like subconsciously we're preparing ourselves for communication with God and, by looking forward to the appointment, we are already having an audience. So the prayer—it's just five or ten minutes—is the formal way of having an audience with God, but this means that all the time, whatever work I am doing, I am always conscious of time and so of my relationship with God. The prayers are so intermingled with our life that we feel that, while enjoying life, we are in constant touch with God.'

I asked him about ritual and the Mufti told me that there were four or five basic rituals in Islam.

'Prayer itself is a ritual. The actions we do—standing up, bowing, prostrating, sitting—these are all rituals, because you don't need to do them. Saying the words should be enough to communicate with God, but word and action is combined.

Ablution—washing hands and face—is like seeking forgiveness from God. We are doing physical things, but we mean spiritual things. Now for the whole of this month, dawn to dusk, we are fasting. It's a funny ritual in that we are *not* doing certain things. By refraining, we are worshipping. Then there's the ritual of money. Two and a half per cent from our saving we give to the poor. It's not out of pity for them, but out of duty towards them. We are worshipping God by giving the money. The final ritual is to go to Mecca.'

I asked how confident the Mufti was that this was the truth, and how important it was to him that other people should believe it.

'This is a very tricky question. We do not claim to be exclusive truth-holders. We think we are continuous with Judaism and Christianity because we think that God communicated with Muhammad directly in continuation with other communications, like in the Torah, Talmud, Old and New Testament. We have to believe in all the books before us, and all the messengers of God before us, and that's why you find hundreds of things common with Judaism and Islam and Christianity also. So in that way we do not think we are new; we are a continuation of the older tradition.'

But the whole truth, he told me, is that because this is the latest revelation, it supersedes the others.

'If it was the same God that sent the message to Moses and Jesus, we will take seriously and act upon this last revelation. Whatever contradiction that exists, we think has developed through the historical process. True religion is always the same.'

THE EASTERN RELIGIONS

I asked him about the Eastern religions.

'Really we are not sure what happened. In the Holy Qur'an it says God did not leave them alone. There were messengers in every single locality on earth. There are certain names mentioned in the holy book that we cannot decipher, so we do not know who they were, so we don't say "Yes" or "No" to anything. We say, "Anything from God is true", without referring to specific revelations or religions. We say, "If it was from God, then we believe it."'

He wanted to add as a final comment:

'We find that in Islam there is a perfect balance between rationality, tradition and ritual. Of course no religion can be without ritualism and without symbolism, but we cannot have that without the rational also. Because there is a frame of reference, there is a text, there is a role model. We can always refer back to it and any deviation and impurities can be checked upon. We do suffer from religious problems, impurities and pollution, but there is always a frame of reference to resolve it and I think that's why there is this clarity of the message, this simplicity, this fine balance between worldly life, tradition, rationality.'

✛

My search for a Muslim woman to talk to led me to London's prestigious Central Mosque and Islamic Cultural Centre in Regent's Park. This complex was built in 1978, largely with money donated by Arab states, and is a remarkable example of Islamic architecture. Dr Fatma Amer, their interfaith representative, arranged a visit for me.

I met Dr Amer in her office. While waiting for her daughter to arrive, the call to worship rang out from the minaret and I asked if I might go and watch the men at prayer from the entrance hall. Men and boys of all ages were streaming in, kicking off their shoes at the door and taking their places in the rows of kneeling figures under an impressive dome, lit by a glorious chandelier.

There were no women in sight. I learnt later that they entered by a different entrance, to a balcony above the hall, to pray.

BASMA ELSHAYYAL

Dr Amer's daughter, Basma, arrived dressed, like her mother, in a full-length skirt and headscarf, somewhat hassled by a dreadful drive across London.

She told me, in perfect English but with an accent I couldn't place, that both her parents were Egyptian and she had been born in Alexandria. Since then she had lived in a variety of places depending on her parents' travels around the world. Basma told me later that most of her formative years had been spent in Scotland. That placed the accent for me! She said:

'Now I consider my allegiance to be first and foremost here. That's my identity. I'm part of the British community.'

Basma is a schoolteacher, head of RE in a north-west London secondary school, where she also teaches citizenship. She is active in quite a few voluntary organizations within the Muslim community—youth initiatives, citizenship, interfaith and women's groups. It was because of this that she had found it useful to cultivate links with the Central Mosque. She didn't have any official role there, although she had taught at the weekend supplementary school in the past.

'At the moment I'm just a regular worshipper. I help out a little, but nothing official. The thing about a mosque is that you don't need to have an officially documented job description to be part of its fabric. You can casually pop in on a Friday, and anyone, after the prayers, can sit down and open a book or ask a question, and if there is someone who can answer it, they will sit down together.'

I asked Basma how her faith made her life better and she replied:

'Firstly it gives me a very clear focus. I know what my ambitions and my goals are. I know what I'm supposed to do in order to get them. It's very helpful that I don't have to answer questions on all sorts of unknown quantities in my life—'Where am I going? Why is this important?'—and so on. It's very comforting to know that everything isn't just down to me, that I'm just one humble, tiny cog in something that's much, much larger and all of that in itself just a tiny speck in the eye of God. I do find that really comforting.'

A HOLISTIC VIEW

She thought that a 'sense of aloneness' was one of the problems, particularly as modern life has speeded up and become so compart-mentalized.

'One really wonderful thing about faith in general, not necessarily just Islam but any faith, is that it gives that holistic view—that you are a human being and part of a greater picture at the same time. You are altogether a person and you have responsi-bilities and duties and privileges and those are divinely given. You're not always having to grapple with a shifting identity or shifting expectations and [having to] renegotiate them every time you meet a new set of people.'

I suggested she was saying that her faith helped her to live well, and she agreed.

'Any faith tells you how to live well, although for me obviously it's Islam, because that's what I have personally experienced. The whole picture is of divine and human relationships and inter-personal dynamics and everything else that goes with it. I think that's really important because there seems a lot of heartache, a lot of insecurity, which can be masked by inappropriate or aggressive behaviour sometimes. Islam provides a framework. There are certain givens, but they're not imposed. It's quite a proactive thing, but these givens do make it quite easy and quite simple to gauge how far you can go, what you can't do and what you can do.'

In practice she found this guidance in the Qur'an.

'I try to look at it directly from the source because I'm very familiar with Arabic. Obviously there are scholars and other people who have written many commentaries and interpretations and so on, and I'll take that into consideration, and something that is really useful is the *Traditions of the Prophet*. Given the fact that he was a person whom everyone loved and admired, it makes natural sense to try to emulate him.'

I asked her about the role of Muslim law and whether, if she couldn't find an answer herself, she would go to a Muslim legal expert.

'Yes, absolutely. I think that's part of my duty and responsibility. Obviously I try my best to live my life according to the laws that I know God has laid down. If you were talking about a legal question, then, because I'm a British citizen, I would discuss it according to British law. However, if it's something to do with personal affairs I would go purely according to what I think God has revealed to me.'

The first goal in Basma's life was 'to be the very best I can be; to try and please God'.

'My major goal would be to live as ethical a life as possible and then everything else would follow from that.'

IF I HAVE TRIED MY BEST

Did she have any goal beyond death?

'I think, if I have tried my best, made the effort to please God, then the natural consequence is that God would be merciful to me and forgiving of my mistakes and sins. Then the hope would be that I would be awarded goodness in the hereafter. However, if I hadn't done as well as I can, hadn't been sincere, then obviously I deserve what's coming. I have to be honest. I don't think every single waking moment of my life, "Am I doing right or wrong?" In this day and age there are other things that occupy our minds—I've run out of petrol; I haven't marked those books; the inspectors are coming in. It's not a constant awareness, which I suppose it should be, but that's life!'

I asked Basma if any reward she received would depend on God's mercy.

'Yes, because I think it would be dreadfully arrogant to say, "Look, I've been so brilliant, I have the right to be admitted into paradise." You can't presume; it makes a bit of a mockery of the whole idea of judgment. It's a superficial example but it's like when students take their A' level exams. You never really know until the results come out.'

HISTORICAL FACTS

Basma was confident in the truth of her religion because she felt that it was based on historical facts.

'For a start, I know that Moses existed and all those prophets and I know that the prophet Mohammed (peace be upon him— upon them all!) existed. That's historical fact, and I know his life was the way it was because there is documentation. So the religion appeals to me logically. It's not that I believe there's something out there somewhere. I look around the world and I can see that God has created this and that's how it is.'

She believed the Qur'an was a direct revelation from God.

'I don't see how else you can explain it, really. It's not the sort of thing that human beings write. I mean, if you read the written

Arabic, certain phraseology is impossible; no human could write it, but you just can't translate it. The first time I read it in English I thought, "This is ridiculous."'

I asked her if she felt she contacted God in her daily life.

'Yes. I do all the time. I think that's one of the things that helps people feel at ease and comfortable, and also it gives some sense of courage. I think the times when you didn't feel the presence of God would be unusual times, because they would be the times when you feel you're all alone—there's nobody there for me; nobody cares—and it's quite a black feeling, until you do remember and snap back to your senses.'

RITUAL

I asked Basma about the place of ritual in her life.

'There are the five daily prayers that I am expected to perform, and I do try and perform those to the best of my ability, when I can.'

Having seen all those men arriving for prayer, I asked her how much, as a woman, she was involved in the daily prayers.

'Men don't have to do it in the hall, as a matter of fact. The legal requirement for men is that they attend the Friday sermon, plus the prayer that follows. Women can attend if they want to.'

Basma argued that the only reason women don't pray in the main hall is because of the availability of space.

'If you go to mosques in other places, like Egypt, you never ever find a balcony except maybe in one or two of the medieval mosques built when space was limited. In all the other main halls, men pray at the front and the women at the back, kids in the middle and that's it. What you see here is just a cultural construct and also, because this is the centre of London, there are some financial reasons here too.'

Basma went on to explain more about the participation of women.

'There are in fact certain situations where women, even though due to their monthly cycle they can't actually pray, are encouraged (in fact they're exhorted) to go and attend celebratory prayers, at Eid, for example.[25] I think women take a very proactive role and it's unfortunate that society has moved on in [such a] way that women are discouraged or made to feel unwelcome sometimes. I actually resent that quite strongly, because the majority of scholars, right up to the late 19th century maybe, would actually have been taught by women. They begin their certifications and qualifications with women teachers, which I think is really important.'

Basma said she believed that she was right in her beliefs.

'I don't *know* I'm right, because obviously there's the human element. In so far as I think my religion is the truth, yes I do, because I feel that I have proof in scriptures; I have proof in the world around me, in what I see.

AN INVITATION

On the question of how important it was to her that other people should believe it too, she said it was like inviting someone to a dinner party.

'You've got this wonderful meal and it's really special and you don't just want to keep it for yourself; you want to invite other people to share it. Now if someone comes along and says, "Well I don't like this" or, "Actually I'm a vegetarian", then you're not going to be mortally offended, because that's their personal choice. You've done your best. The translation of *da'wah*[26] is actually 'invitation'. If people want to come, then you're very happy and make them welcome, but if they don't, that's their decision and that's the end of the story.'

To Christians she wanted to say two things.

'The first one would be that I can't be a decent Muslim unless I believe with all my heart in God and his prophets and his books and the day of judgment and so on. Given that I believe in the prophets, that automatically means that I believe in Adam, Moses and Jesus, and if I believe in God's books, I automatically believe in the Torah, the Old and the New Testaments because that's part of my faith.

'The second thing is that just as you've got an entire spectrum of Christians—Catholic, Orthodox, Protestants and so forth, and you've got the very historical view of Christianity and the more modern—it's the same in Islam. So I think it's important, for everybody, to appreciate the fact that Islam has a huge, wide spectrum. Islam is enriched by a lot of cultural interaction. In the spread of Islam the whole issue is not just of tolerance but positive interaction.'

KHADIJAH ELSHAYYAL

Basma's sister Khadijah had come in and joined us at the table. She told me that she too tries to make Islam the basis of her life, so that it gives her a purpose behind everything she does. When making decisions she asks herself what would make her a better Muslim.

'It gives a flavour to life. The thing about sharing faith with other people is that you know you're always in good company, wherever you go. I may be following a different career path from my best friend but we know that we're doing what we're doing for

the same reasons. Shared acts of faith make you feel part of
something wider and give you strength and support.'

*Basma walked with me through the spacious courtyard of the complex,
where people stood and chatted in the evening light and small boys played
on their bikes, back on to Park Road to find the bus home.*

One of London's new universities—the Metropolitan—has a
building in the shell of an old warehouse in the Whitechapel area
of East London. I went there to meet a member of the academic
staff, a colleague of a friend from church. Habib Rahman came to
the university to teach computing on a business course, but is now
mostly involved in recruitment and in providing advice and
guidance to undergraduate students.

I was shown to his office, where he welcomed me with a cup
of tea. He told me that many Bangladeshis arrive in England with
qualifications that they can't use and the younger generation often
don't take the opportunities they are offered at school, so the
university has an advice and counselling centre, which has resulted
in their now having around five hundred Bangladeshi students on
undergraduate courses at the university.

HABIB RAHMAN

*I asked Habib about his religious background and he said that he had
been born in Bangladesh into a Muslim family which had encouraged him
in the faith and practice of Islam, but he didn't really have much of an
education in the religion.*

'In your early days you go to the mosque and learn how to read
the Qu'ran. Most Muslims can read the Qu'ran but not understand it and that was pretty much the case with us.'

Habib came to England when he was twelve and has been part of the East London Muslim community ever since. He is now the secretary of the mosque in Whitechapel.

'Fortunately for me, because I was part of this community, I had the opportunity of understanding my religion and way of life.'

I asked him how he thought his life was better because he was a Muslim.

'Both the Qu'ran and the Sunnah[27] give you guidance on your life and that dictates how you relate to others, how you behave, the outlook you have on [this] life and the life after. So I think it makes me more reflective. Having my own extended family, my own children, I'm always thinking, "What is the best way of doing this?" Islam teaches you about every aspect of the things you do.'

He felt that the rituals of Islam were also something you could reflect on and ask, 'How does that make me a better person?'

'One of the things that the Qu'ran says is that praying keeps you from all kinds of wrong and shameful deeds. When you're in a state of worship, you don't think of doing bad things. So early in the morning you get up to pray, although you don't really feel like it, and that starts your day in a good way. Then a little later, come lunchtime, there's another prayer. So it's a continuous reminder.'

A RESPONSIBILITY

Habib thought Islam helped people face the traumas of life.

'All kinds of bad things happen around you and in the world. Islam is a very practical way of life so it recognizes that these problems will be there. It's understood that the purpose in our being here is that we are being tested by God. You may have a calamity in your life and you can say, "God has really given me this horrific test, and it's really unfair", or you patiently persevere and say, "Well, OK, I accept that and there will be something better afterwards."

I enquired what the ultimate goal of his religious life was.

'Well, what the Qu'ran teaches is that you are looking for the pleasure of God. You are trying to do the best that you can within your means. We ask God to give us the best in this life and in the life hereafter. The good pleasure of God in this life is that you have a fairly contented life, and then beyond this life you are looking for his mercy rather than his wrath, and therefore admission into the gardens rather than hellfire.'

REPENTANCE AND FORGIVENESS

Habib was well aware of our failings and our continual need for forgiveness.

'One of the things we believe is that our good actions are not necessarily adequate to get the good pleasure of God, because we make so many wrong actions at the same time. So if somebody says, "I'm counting on my good deeds", I don't think it's going to work because of our failings. One of the strongest principles in Islam is that you repent and you ask forgiveness. That door is open until your very last breath.'

Was he saying that it all depended on God's mercy and God gives his mercy to those who make an effort?

'To those who deserve it, yes, absolutely. If you know what you're supposed to do and you defy God, defiance is not something that's going to deserve mercy.'

So at the moment you don't know what your eternal destiny will be?

'Absolutely, I'm hoping and I'm working towards it. God is merciful.'

I asked Habib about how the message of Islam comes to us and he said that he believed it was a natural process from the creation of the world.

'What the Qu'ran says is that after creating men and putting them on earth, God promised them guidance. He said that from time to time guidance would come and those who follow will have nothing to worry about. We believe that from the day of Adam to Muhammad there's been a chain of prophets. The Qu'ran also mentions that to every nation there has come a prophet; every nation has had the opportunity of guidance from the creator. "Islam" literally means submission to God. Muslims believe that this is what all the prophets practised and taught.'

Might there have been another chain of prophets in the Eastern nations?

'That's not what I'm saying. What I'm saying is that every nation has had some guidance from God, and it would have been in the same stream. At times there were several prophets in different regions at the same time, but there would have been a consistency in the guidance that came from God.'

SERENITY AND PEACE

I asked him if he felt some sort of personal contact with God. He said he did but it was difficult to say how it manifested itself.

'Certainly the feeling that you get and the serenity or the peace that you feel, I think that would be the way that you could say that there is some contact. If you have a lot of problems then you leave everything and you go and do a prayer and you get engrossed in your prayer, and that gives you a different kind of feeling and you feel that your burden's lightened. So it's a kind of relationship that you build with God.'

Do you ask God for things?

'Absolutely, all the time. The most common thing we ask God for is forgiveness—we make so many mistakes—but then you say, "Protect my children; don't give us any vile illnesses" and so on. The Prophet recommends supplications for everything that you do, when you go to sleep, when you get up, when you leave your home. A lot of the time it can be about physical things, and you can ask for things for the life hereafter. You want his grace and you want his mercy and you want to go to heaven. I think in Islam we believe that not everything will be granted to us immediately, necessarily, [as] it may not be the best for us, but your supplications are not wasted.'

I had one last question. How certain was he that his religion is the truth and how important was it that other people should see it too?

'I think, as belief goes, there can't be any wavering. I'm absolutely certain that it's the truth and I think it's also important for me, in a nice way, to convey it to others. If you think you have the opportunity to go to heaven and others are not going to heaven, you have a duty to tell them.'

A MISSIONARY RESPONSIBILITY

'Muslims have a missionary responsibility. The Prophet has told us to do it and also shown us how it is to be done. The Qu'ran makes it very clear that there is no compulsion in religion, so you can't force people to become Muslims. What you can do is to say that this is a way of life, and this is good for you and we believe that this is the truth, and then we leave it to the individual to accept it or not. Muslims need to show what Islam is in their practice, rather than me sitting here and saying, "You have to take this as the truth, otherwise you're going to hell." That's not the way and that's not how it's been propagated in the past. Muslims have gone to different parts of the world; they've done business there; people have seen their dealings; they've married into those communities and people naturally accepted Islam. They saw it to be a different and better way of life.'

I had finished with my questions but I asked him if he wanted to say anything else to Christians about their attitudes to people from other faiths.

'Not so much about their attitudes; I think more about their understanding. What people see to be a religion and the practice of a religion may not necessarily be so. I think that is especially true when it comes to Islam. In the media Islam is hijacked to all intents and purposes. A few people misrepresent Islam in a way the majority would condemn, but still you will find that's the view that people have. So Islam may be perceived to be very arrogant, very hostile, very violent, and that is not the case. People who have lived and worked with Muslims who actually practise their religion have a better understanding of what Islam is from the shared experience. From these [experiences] perhaps will come out things which will be beneficial to all of us.'

SOME REFLECTIONS

I met Muslims from India, from Egypt and from Bangladesh, although they had all been largely educated in Britain. These are three quite different cultures, but I felt there was a consistency in their thoughts and feelings about their religion.

Mufti Battula found 'solace and tranquillity' in it. He told me that he was 'at peace with God'. It gave 'serenity and peace' to Habib, and Basma found it 'comforting'. It was helpful, she said, that she didn't have to find her own answers to questions like 'Where am I?' or 'What am I supposed to do?' Habib was sure that understanding the purpose of our lives helped people to face the traumas of life, to accept and use suffering when it came. When you pray about your problems, he said, 'the burden is lightened'.

In each conversation I noticed the appreciation of a clear sense of direction. 'I know what I am supposed to do,' said Basma. The religion gave them a shared framework, a structure for a disciplined, harmonious, satisfying life, and hope for the future.

The Mufti spoke of the continual ritual of prayer being 'the essential organizer of our lives'. To Habib it was a 'continuous reminder'. 'It starts in the morning and goes through to the evening through your entire life and affects everything that you do.'

All three were clear that their goal was to live a life that pleased God, in the hope of receiving his mercy. 'One of the strongest principles in Islam,' Habib said, 'is that you repent and ask for forgiveness.' The Mufti said, 'It is by the mercy of God alone that we will be able to achieve any goal or object", and they lived in hope, but not in certainty, because they believed that God's mercy is offered not to the defiant but to the sincere, even if they fail.

It came out quite strongly that mission was an obligation, but also seen as an invitation (like asking someone to a dinner party, said Basma), and that they see their religion as part of a continuous stream with Judaism and Christianity. 'We do not claim to be exclusive truth holders,' the Mufti told me; 'we are continuous with Judaism and Christianity' but he added that 'the whole truth is that because this is the latest revelation, it supersedes the others'. He and Habib both mentioned that the Qur'an said God had sent messengers to 'every single locality on earth' and Basma and Habib both wanted Christians to appreciate the diversity within Islam, which they felt had been 'hijacked by the media'.

CHAPTER 11

LISTENING TO SIKHS

When I telephoned the Sikh Gurdwara in Kingsbury, it was Harkesh Kapoor, a volunteer helper, who answered the phone. When I explained what I was looking for, he said immediately that he would like to talk to me himself. This cheerful friendliness and enthusiasm to share their faith was, I discovered later, characteristic of all the Sikhs I met. I went to his home one evening and we talked about Sikhism over a glass of lemonade.

HARKESH KAPOOR

Harkesh had been brought up as a Sikh in India and got to know London well, travelling with his father who was in the Indian Foreign Service. He now stays regularly in London and helps out at the Gurdwara when he can.

'This is in a way a free service; it is a way of prayer, a way of worshipping.'

Harkesh began by telling me that Sikhism began in the 15th century and was basically an offshoot of Hinduism. He said that Hinduism had been getting caught up in ritualism and was going astray from the truth. It was to eradicate this that the foundations of modern-day Sikhism were laid by the first of the ten Gurus, Guru Nanak.

'Guru Nanak Dev Ji was completely non-sectarian. He had two disciples throughout his life. One was a Hindu and the other was a

Muslim, who was a musical instrument player. There are hymns by Muslims in our holy book, the Adi Granth Sahib.'[28]

I asked him how he thought being a Sikh made his life better and he said it gave him a path to God and a view of something to look forward to in eternity.

'Sikhism also gives you a guideline, and it depends on the individual how much you create love for the religion. The more you create love for the religion, the more the religion is within you, the more it brings you the light, the sight, the more it gives you a goal—shows you what you have to achieve—the more it binds you so that you have to stick with it.'

Sikhism gave to Harkesh a way of contacting God, of finding his comfort and strength for his daily life.

'It is that "non-mind" or "non-thoughtness", which is called the eternal silence, that gives you the power, the courage and, most importantly, the peace of mind to fight your way through the bad things in the world.'

I asked him what he thought the human problem basically was and he said it was that we ignore our consciences.

'If you take any action, your mind will give you a reason for it, but your conscience will tell you whether this is right or wrong. Our mind tries to subjugate our conscience. That's why they say, "Listen to your conscience!"'

He thought that our conscience was God in us.

'It is him. In my religion they say we are God; we have a part of him within us.'

When I enquired about the goal of his life, he told me:

'I've taken it upon myself to be a devout servant of God and help as many people as I can, in the way of introducing them to their soul, by telling them the truth, by passing on what I've learnt to as many people as possible.'

Harkesh felt, however, that he would probably think, at the end of his life, that he had not done even one single good deed.

'I personally feel that if God accepts me as his servant, I should be really fortunate to have his grace.'

He told me that he believed in 'life after life'.

'It's not just because my elders have said it, but because in every association that I've made with everyone, there seems to be a touch from behind. It's all our past deeds and it's quite a good justification for the idea that our actions do get counted.'

IT COMES WITH HIS GRACE

I asked him if he was, then, hoping for another life?

'My hope is not for another life; the ultimate aim is to get salvation, not to come again, because coming in this world is misery. Salvation is an unachievable thing because as a human being it's not possible. It comes with his grace, but [in another way] I would wish to come again and again, because the achievement and eternal joy you get when you pray to him is unsurmountable and I would like to repeat the procedure in my lives.'

I asked him what part prayer and meditation played in the practice of his religion.

'What our religion says is—pray! The only thing that we have in our hands is prayer. We can only pray to God, that God forgive us. "God grant me your name; grant me the company of your people." If you are a good human being and you pray with utmost humbleness, he always listens. In our religion we say that he is closer to us than even our hands and feet. It's only for us to visualize how close he is. In Sikhism the only way to God is *naam*.'

Harkesh then explained to me the Sikh idea of naam.

'It means recitation of God's name. Whatever name you give to God you can recite, and that is the achievement of your goal. When you are repeating it, it is actually controlling all the five senses. It creates a oneness within you. You lose yourself and you get something else. It creates solitude in your mind; it creates peace in you.'

I asked him if he prayed for specific things.

'Never, never. Why? Because he has given so many things by himself that we haven't asked for. Learned people say you shouldn't ever ask him for something, because he probably doesn't wish that for you, and he probably takes away some other things and gives you the things you're asking for. Then ultimately you say, "I was better off without it", but this really is not easy to come by. It's a learning process.'

PRAYER AND MEDITATION

'Prayer and meditation go hand in hand. When you are in the initial classes of spirituality, things you say from your lips are your prayer, but when it comes from the depth of your heart or feeling, it becomes a meditation. You need not sit for hours or [take up] any difficult positions to do this. It's one of the easiest things, but yes, it comes more easily if you go on practising it. You can do this even while you are doing your work. You can still think of him with warmth and love. It is a profound feeling. It is an essential ingredient of sound religion.'

Did he feel that he contacted God at times like this?

'I wouldn't say that for sure, but I am starting to have this kind of feeling, that he does contact you and that he does save you from so many things. I'm fortunate enough to have his grace that he has been with me all the time, in the sense that he saves me from going astray. Yes, I really do feel his presence with me.'

WORSHIPPING THE WORDS OF GOD

I asked him about worship and he told me:

'In our religion you don't need to worship a picture, a person or a book. You need to worship the words of God, his commands, and basically that's what is written in this compilation of our Gurus, the Adi Granth Sahib.'

To show me why this was important, he said it was like a person standing on a terrace.

'This person says, "Come up the stairs and see me", and that person who was standing down there, comes up the stairs and meets him. So what is strong? Is it that person or is it his words? It is the words that have guided him to the goal. So in our religion it is the valuable words, it is the hymns of different religious saints, sufis and Gurus, which are compiled together in the form of the *Guru Granth Sahib*. The Gurus commanded us to follow the words of the holy book. They said, "You don't need to go anywhere else. This is your Guru. This is your God."'

Most of their ritual surrounds the book.

'In a symbolic way we treat the book as a living God. Waking up, we put on beautiful clothes and place it on a pedestal, take the first words as the command for the day and sing hymns in front of it. In the evening, when we finish our prayers, we let it sleep. It brings you closer to the power and makes you feel that God is present with you in your daily life. You see, a person is very weak. We all need a shoulder where we can put our head and seek support and solace. A man seeks his wife's shoulder; a wife seeks her man's, a son his father and a daughter her mother; and when things go beyond that we seek a holy man's shoulder to help us through. The learned person that we seek is our Guru Granth Sahib. We listen to it and it gives us live examples of what is right and wrong. We draw inspiration and solace from it. It gives us the courage to stand up and fight.'

I asked him about his own reading of the book and he said:

'I read it whenever I get the chance. I'm not very learned. I was never taught Punjabi but the love to read it made me learn. I wouldn't say I'm capable of understanding every word but I do get the crux of it and there are elders I can ask for help, but the amazing thing is that over and over again upon reading, the message gets clearer and more forthright.'

I introduced the question of other faiths.

'Our tenth and last Guru, Guru Gobind Singh Ji, wrote a prayer that we recite every day as part of our daily ritual. "God has created diversity. God has created unending diverse ways, but yet he is one." This is unity in diversity. He did this because he was so great. If we were all the same and all talked the same, it would be a monotonous and very boring society. The beauty of society is that we are different and we still live together.'

Harkesh felt that all the religions have the same goal.

'They all try to make you a better human being, more humane, more conscious, more tolerant, more truth-seeking. Every place had a different prophet. If it was Lord Muhammad, if it was Lord Jesus, if it was Lord Krishna—they are all his sons. They were all sent by him. He has spoken at different times, to different people, in different languages and in different places, but the message was the same.'

THE PATHS ARE DIFFERENT BUT THE GOAL IS THE SAME

'What God has done is give us all different visions and different experiences. The true path to God for me might not be the true path for you. You can never say that the path is the same for all. The paths are different, but the goal is the same. What I feel is true for me is not necessarily true for you too. It is this diversity that a man should understand. It is the respect and tolerance for all paths that gives immense happiness to me. Once people understand, I think all the problems of these inter-religious discrepancies, these clashes of faiths, will end.'

I pressed him with a question about truth in religion, but he ended by saying:

'Unfortunately you've come to a person who believes all religions are the same. I personally feel there is no difference in any religion.'

So you think it's better if people stay in the religion they're in?

'I would go one step further: I would say people are more fortunate if they are in the better surroundings of their respective religion. Every religion has its better and worse sides.'

After more lemonade and some very good Indian sweets, we said our goodbyes and I went back out into a wet December night to find the underground station and the train home.

GURCHARAN SINGH

I got talking to Gurcharan Singh at a meeting of the Interfaith Centre in Kilburn. There was a break for refreshments and, as we chatted, I told him about the book I was writing. He was eager to take part and talk to me about his faith. He had come to England in 1962, to further his education, with his three brothers. They are instrumentalists and singers and they lead the worship in several London Gurdwaras. He told me:

'Singing is the core of the Sikh faith. Guru Nanak has described music as a means of attaining spiritual joy and transcendental bliss.'

He arranged for me to meet him and a young Sikh woman, Harjit Kaur, at his home in Wembley. The Christmas tree, he explained with a smile when he showed me in, was 'because we have grandchildren'.

Although born in India, Gurcharan had spent most of his childhood in Uganda and he talked to me about the problems they faced when they arrived in England.

'It was very cold and I found a big difference in culture. Africa was like a time capsule. There Hindus, Sikhs and Muslims lived in harmony with each other. They were not affected by the partition of India or the politics of the sub-continent. There was no animosity between us. We maintained our identity and we were proud of what we were. When we came to this country we were exposed to different political and religious views. We found [that] people from India and Pakistan were different from us. What worried me was that they made people aware of their religion. That hurt, because to me religion is something very peaceful and if someone has distress because of religion then something is wrong.'

If God is the creator of each and every one, he argued, then there shouldn't be fear. We should believe in and accept 'the universal brother-hood'. Gurcharan went on to say that things had improved now.

'In early days there was a lot of discrimination from the host community towards Sikhs—due to ignorance about our faith and outlook.'

GURCHARAN AND HARJIT KAUR

Harjit then arrived and introduced herself as a family friend. Gurcharan's son, she told me, is teaching her to play the harmonium. It was the first time I had seen a woman wearing the familiar Sikh turban, and she looked quite splendid in it. Born and raised in Wolverhampton, she was now at university in London. I began by asking her how her faith made her life better.

'I think it gives a stability in life. Having moved away from my family, having come to London, where I have no connections at all, it provides some sort of inner strength to me because it's so chaotic here, studying and just living actually. It brings me a calmness. I don't believe I am alone, ever.'

Harjit said that a lot of her friends who were not into Sikhism, or had no religion at all, tended to stray when they got to London.

'They get a bit messed up because they think they're all alone. They think there's no one there who cares, while because I believe that whatever I do I'm being protected, because I have faith in that, I'm more stable, I'm more secure with myself.'

Gurcharan added:

'Life is lonely and you need some sort of support. We are physical beings, you know, dust to dust and ashes to ashes, but also we are part of a very big spiritual power. To me, to believe in God and to meditate on his virtues gives me my strength and it gives me the goal of my life as well.'

I asked them about the problems of living a human life. Harjit thought that one of them is that everyone is always busy.

'People have their own lives to lead; they are always self-complete. It's very much a case of "It's my own life; I don't have any issues with anyone else." It's just ego, and because of that there are a lot of problems today—like everything that's happened with America and the Palestinians.'

PROVIDING TOLERANCE FOR TODAY'S WORLD

She continued:

'Our religion is about love and the acceptance of everybody else. It has always been a matter of "They have a different religion; they have a different practice, but they're still praying to the one God"—which is what we are doing as well, maybe in a different way, but everyone should have the freedom to do what they please. I think that's what Sikhism has provided for the modern world.'

Gurcharan added:

'When you look at our hymns it's all compassion, love, community service; and the Sikh faith gives you humbleness—that's very important. Ego or "I-am-ness" is the major cause of conflicts within families, communities and religions. Guru Nanak's message is a guideline to the true path which leads towards oneness with God and hence strengthening universal brotherhood as well.'

Harjit wanted to point out that this idea of brotherhood included women.

'In India, at the time of Guru Nanak, women were treated as men's property. There was the burning of the wife when the husband died and Guru Nanak put a stop to that. There's a famous quote in the Guru Granth Sahib where he asks, "Why insult women when they give birth to kings and they can break or make a nation?" That's very true. In fact, I think Guru Nanak put women on a higher level than any other faith has ever done, not equal but even higher. He said they can make or break a nation because they are the ones who bring up the children and instil the main morals and principles in the young, so that stands out about Sikhism compared with other religions. It makes a point of saying that women have a status; they have a role to play.'

Gurcharan agreed and explained that in Sikhism women can play a full part in all the ceremonies. There is no role in the religion that they are excluded from.

CONNECTING WITH GOD

I then asked them both about the goal of their religious life, and Harjit answered first.

'I think we see God in everything and you find a bit of God within yourself. My aim is to be one with God. Our role models are our Gurus because they gave the message. They had God within them and they had connected to God themselves and through them God spoke. We aspire to be very much like them, to lead a good life so that one day we can all connect with God.'

She explained that life could be very mundane if you just lived it, got up, worked, went to sleep.

'There's no purpose to it. Because we have this cycle of human lives, my aim is to break the cycle, through prayer and meditation, and connect with God.'

I asked Gurcharan if he felt that God was with him in his daily life.

'Yes, I think that's what gives me strength, because it's not just prayers five times a day. The secret of life is that you should remember God all the time—basically you breathe the name of God all the time. You need to take the ego out of prayer so you aren't conscious of praying.'

He then told me a story recounted by a Sikh saint.

'A saint of ours tells the story of a man who was working hard. "Why are you so engrossed with your own work? Why do you worship God so seldom?" another man asked him. He said, "Look, have you realized that it's your conscious brain which keeps on working?" He gave as an example, "When a lady takes a pitcher on her head, she walks and talks, but the pitcher doesn't fall. A mother can do the cooking and all that, yet her mind is always with the son she is looking after." So unconsciously you are meditating. In the morning you pray and that's like a kind of kick-start. Then the rest of the day you can be in tune with God all the time.'

Remembering Harkesh's emphasis on their book, I asked Harjit what their holy book meant to her.

'I think, in all honesty, that it has all the answers. Over two hundred years there were ten Gurus that came down and they've given us everything we need to know to become one with God.'

Gurcharan wanted to tell me that another thing about the Sikh faith is that anyone who comes in to support it is expected to protect it.

'Guru Gobind Singh said he would create a person—a saint/soldier—who could be identified, whom people could call on when they were in trouble, who would be compassionate, loving and protective. When the crunch came, Sikhs kept the sword. This is for protection and to give them confidence. The Sikh faith is very passive, but at the same time, to protect it, you should stand for your God.'

I asked Gurcharan how important the other outward signs of Sikhism[29] were for today.

'I think the Gurus said it because it is very, very important. They remind you that you should live in the will of God. [The ruling] was made so that if anyone could see a Sikh, they could always go for help. It represents the Sikh values and that's why we do it. With Sikh youngsters it keeps them from the wrong things. If you wear a turban you think twice about smoking or doing wrong. If a Sikh does something wrong, they can be picked out— "he did it!" It makes you careful.'

WEARING A TURBAN

Harjit agreed. She was born in England but still feels that if you can't discipline the outside, there is no way you can achieve inner discipline.

'That's one of the reasons I wear a turban. I started wearing it when I came to university about three years ago and it was because, without it, I would mingle in a crowd and no one would know I'm a Sikh. Our faith is not a men's only faith. There are not certain rules for men and others for women. When Guru Gobind Singh gave the Sikh identity, he gave it to the Sikh faith, not to the Sikh men. I wear a turban because I know that from a million people I will stick out. It helps me in my life because if I do wrong, not only will my reputation be tarnished but I will tarnish everyone else's, and I won't be responsible for that; it's too much of a burden.'

I asked how important it was to them that other people found this way of life, and Harjit said:

'We have the stability of believing in God, and a lot of Sikhs exude the confidence other people want. That's why we don't believe in forced conversions because our religion says that if you can live your life as a Sikh in the best possible way, then everyone else will be drawn to you. They will want to know why you are always smiling, never get depressed. People will want to know, because they lack that in their lives, so then they'll learn more about your religion.'

She told me that she believed that every religion leads to God, but added:

'I think our religion (I'm a bit biased here) is an easier way. You don't have to do certain things at certain times of day. There's nothing so strict about it; anyone can follow it. If people want to come to our religion, that's fine, and they do it of their own accord. We don't believe in conversion.'

Gurcharan added:

'One thing I don't like is when people try to justify their faith by downgrading other faiths. This is rather sad. We used to have a Christian evangelist come here. I said to him, "Look, I will become a Christian, no problem. You tell me what it has to offer me." If [a religion] gives you love and compassion and a standing for justice, it doesn't matter what religion it is. I think that religions of grace will always be here. You will keep with your own religion because you can understand it. If I ask you to become a Sikh, there are two problems—[firstly] because you don't know Punjabi, and [so, secondly] the joy I get from playing this music with my own hands and singing these hymns wouldn't be possible for you At the end of the day a religion should make you a better person; that's what the whole of religion is about. Where nature places you is your stepping-stone.'

Gurcharan had mentioned 'religions of grace' so I asked him to say more about the place of grace in Sikhism.

'In the Sikh faith, the grace of God is crucial. In achieving the goal it is very, very important. You cannot achieve ultimate union with the Almighty without his grace. This is said again and again; without his grace we should fail, and that's why we say, "Ask for grace all the time", because he is the provider. He can give you leeway in worldly things, like you can work hard and fall in love and win someone, but to be one with him, that cannot be without his grace. That is the "underlying" of the Sikh faith.'

During the interview, Gurcharan's wife had brought in tea and freshly cooked vegetable rolls. Wonderful as they were, I couldn't possibly eat them all, so I set off home with them in a bag for my grandchildren's tea.

SOME REFLECTIONS

I was quite moved to hear Gurcharan's emphasis on grace as the 'underlying'—the foundation—of the Sikh faith, and Harkesh said too that salvation was 'an unachievable thing'. 'As a human it's not possible,' he said. 'It comes with his grace.'

I was interested too in Harkesh's remarks about the beginnings of Sikhism. People have made a comparison between this religion, begun in India by Guru Nanak (who died in 1539), and Protestant Christianity, begun in Germany by Martin Luther (who died in

1546). Both men tried to transform a religion that had become bound by ritual into a religion set free by grace—a religion that had become remote and dull into a religion based on an intense, personal relationship with God. Harkesh said that his religion was a way of contacting God, of finding his comfort and strength for his daily life, Gurcharan that it was 'the path which leads to oneness with God', and Harjit said the Gurus were her models because 'they had connected with God'.

We can perhaps see here the influence of the devotional strand of Hinduism, where the divine is seen as a unique and personal Lord (usually visualized as either Krishna or Rama). The deep love of a pure and humble heart, expressed in outward devotion, is answered by grace and the gift of liberation from the round of birth and rebirth. Although there is a sense of helplessness, the element of mercy (as the Semitic religions understand it) is not usually very strong in Hinduism, but Harkesh said, 'The only thing we have in our hands is prayer. We can only pray to God, that God forgives us.' He said he would feel at the end of his life that he had not done even one good deed and felt that he would be 'really fortunate' to have God's grace. Other influences of both Christianity and Islam can perhaps be seen in the rejection of image-worship and the emphasis on the book as the source of guidance for life.

Reincarnation was there: salvation for Harkesh was 'not to come again' and for Harjit 'to break the cycle', but the ultimate goal for all of them was this sense of connecting with God, of being one with him, not just as an idea but as an experience.

I noticed again the problem with the 'ego'—what Gurcharan called 'I-am-ness' and saw as 'the major cause of conflicts, within the family, the community and between religions'. It was, he said, Guru Nanak's message that was the answer to it—'a guideline to the true path to oneness with God and hence to the strengthening of universal brotherhood'. This emphasis on the message was reflected in Harkesh's interesting comments about worshipping not the book, but the words of God, which had the power to draw people to 'come and see'.

Did you notice too that 'the secret of life', according to Gurcharan, is that we should remember God, breathe the name of God, all the time? Harkesh spoke of the practice of *naam*—the recitation of God's name—as something in which you lose yourself and find solitude and peace. This picks up much that we have heard before, and Gurcharan added the interesting comment that you need to take the ego out of prayer, so that you aren't conscious of praying. You can then, he said, 'be in tune with God all the time'.

Harjit said Sikhs didn't believe in conversion and Gurchuran felt it was sad when people tried to justify their own religion by downgrading other faiths. Harkesh, like several others before, believed that God had 'spoken at different times to different people in different places', and had intentionally created this diversity, 'because he was so great'.

These are just some of the ideas that I hope we can take with us as we start to think about our responses to these conversations.

TALKING ABOUT JESUS
IN THE WORLD TODAY

INTRODUCTION

In many ways I want you, the reader, to make your own response to this material. Everyone comes to it from a different background and with a different perspective. It has had quite an impact on me, however, and I would like firstly to share with you my own reactions to it, and then to outline the range of views that Christians hold about other faiths and discuss how the Church might move forward on this subject.

This will take two chapters. In the third and last chapter in this final section, I will consider the challenge to Christians to talk about Jesus in our world today, and then draw out from these conversations some ideas about how it might be done.

CHAPTER 12

WHAT CAN WE SAY ABOUT PEOPLE OF OTHER FAITHS?

I hope you found the rich tapestry of ideas, practices and experiences revealed in the last section as stimulating as I did, as I went around meeting and talking with this fascinating mixture of London people. Many moments and phrases have stayed fresh in my memory. I am left with the general feeling of different coloured threads—righteousness and enlightenment, revelation, grace and mercy, ritual and prayer, guidance and comfort, judgment, redemption, liberation and future bliss, meaninglessness, isolation and pain, peace and harmony, egoism and greed, friendship and community, diversity and truth—weaving around each other in different strengths and combinations through the various conversations.

At times I admit I felt intimidated and confused by the complexity of all this material but, encouraged by so many of the participants, I have found celebration and praise to be an equally possible, and a much more positive, response.

We began the first section of this book by looking at some of the things that Christians say about people of other faiths and, now that we have listened to some of these people, we need to go back and ask if we can go on saying things like this. We dearly want to go on talking about Jesus, but how best can we now do it without seeming to have our heads in the sand and without discrediting the faith we so much want to commend? Here are some of the reactions I had to these conversations. I hope they may help you to think through your own.

CHRISTIAN UNIQUENESS

Christianity has, from its beginnings, stressed its uniqueness and universality. The early Christians believed that in Jesus something new and of cosmic significance had happened and the call to respond to this event was urgent and decisive. These are still very important elements in our faith, but how shall we talk about this event now, in today's multi-cultural, multi-faith world?

Some Christians say that Christianity is unique among the world religions because it is about God revealing himself to us rather than people trying to think it through for themselves, or because it's about the divine coming to earth in human form. I would suggest that we have seen that this is just not true. Christianity is certainly unique but it is not unique in either of these respects. Our conversations have shown that all the other five major world religions contain claims of eternal truth being revealed from other realms, and many of the people within them treat their scriptures with enormous respect. Several of those I talked to spoke of people from the past being 'God with us' in many different ways. How can we respond to claims like these, which are not the same as ours in every detail, but as strong and as sincerely believed, and coming with just the sort of authority we claim for the sources of our own faith?

ARE ONLY OUR CLAIMS AUTHENTIC?

We might say that only our claims are authentic and that people who take other writings and other figures for their authority about the real meaning of life are mistaken, and therefore in error about what they discover. After the conversations I had, however, I would not feel at all happy about saying this. I would be declaring my own faith but on what basis could I decry the faith of others? If I wanted to go down this road I would want there to be some objective argument to support the idea that the revelation in which I put my trust is the only reliable one. It surely won't do simply to argue,

'This one is the best because it's what I believe.' After all, people of other faiths do say exactly the same, and at an interfaith group I attended, someone pointed out that almost all religious people are in the religion of their birth, and think that they have freely chosen it.

If we want to find some independent criteria for claiming that our revelation is the only authentic one, where shall we look? Christianity has a remarkable history of survival, adaptability and growth, but so do Buddhism and Islam. Christianity has inspired remarkable moves forward in humanitarian concern, but also remarkable steps backwards in cruelty and oppression. Christianity has produced some impressive, internationally known saints, but so, for example, has Hinduism. On any objective method one might propose for finding the best religion in the world, no one of these six seems obviously to stand out from the others.

This is not about suspending our sense of values and saying that all religions are the same or that they all help people live better lives. Religions are not all the same, and some forms of them do not help people live better lives. One issue that I think has come over very strongly in these conversations is the diversity within these six religions, which have developed over centuries and within some very different cultures. We do not need to agree in detail on sets of values to see that some forms of religions, even of the six we have been looking at, including Christianity, are restrictive and oppressive and lead to fearful, diminished lives, while some are liberating and empowering and lead to rich and satisfying lives, even if they are still lived in trying and painful circumstances.

Trying to argue for the superiority of any one of these major world faiths over the others on the ground of any objective evidence seems, to me, doomed to failure.

ARE ONLY OUR EXPERIENCES GENUINE, ONLY OUR PRAYERS ANSWERED?

Another way of arguing for the unique authority of the sources of our religion is to say that I know my religion is true because it works for me; I have tried it as a way of finding reconciliation with God, with other people and with myself, and my own experience tells me that it works. It is true! Have we not, however, just been reading similar claims for other ways—claims of having found peace with God, of 'connecting' with him, of inspiration and strength for holy living, of confidence in prayer, hope for the future and a real sense of God's presence around and within? So is only my experience and my testimony genuine? Listening to these conversations over the past few months, I have been most impressed by the stories of answered prayer that sound so like my own—God responding to my requests with healing, guidance and peace.

Can I suggest that if the understanding of our faith leads us to reject these testimonies (perhaps because we believe Jesus said he was 'the only way'), we have moved a long way from the faith of Jesus, the Bible and the historic teaching of the Church. Old Testament saints like Abraham, Moses and Elijah testified of knowing God and of walking through life with him, and the New Testament testifies to their having received his salvation.[30] All through both Testaments, men and women turn up from outside the covenant people and their knowledge of God is recognized and commended —Melchizedek, Jethro, Balaam and Balak, Rahab, the wise men in the nativity story, Cornelius and an unnamed Roman centurion.[31] Whatever Jesus meant when he said to his disciples that he was the only way, clearly he didn't mean that only those who have a personal faith in his death for them, or have been baptized into his Church, can know God or receive his gift of salvation.

DO ONLY CHRISTIANS DEPEND ON GRACE?

We noted at the beginning that some Christians say their religion is the only religion of grace. The last conversation alone is enough to prove this to be simply untrue. I was surprised at how often, quite unprompted, the word 'grace' was mentioned. It does not of course always mean exactly the same thing, but the idea of an unmerited gift from a divine being was always there. In the Semitic religions, where the problem is often seen as the gap between a holy God and unholy people, the gift is firstly mercy, and then all that comes under the immensely rich idea of 'salvation'. In the Eastern religions, where the problem is often seen more as a matter of ignorance or misperception, grace tends to be about an unmerited gift of enlightenment, of liberation from the things that bind us into the cycle of life; but having said that, forgiveness came over strongly in my conversations about grace in Sikhism.[32]

I can hear some enthusiastic Protestants saying, 'Yes, but only Christianity is about grace *alone*.' Many of us can appreciate the need for this emphasis at the time of the Reformation, and whenever pride starts to creep into our relationship with God, but surely we can see, from the Bible, that people can exclude themselves from God's grace by being too proud, defiant, lazy, self-centred or unforgiving.[33] Paul said, 'I press on towards the goal to win the prize for which God has called me heavenwards in Christ Jesus' (Philippians 3:14). It is very interesting to compare the ideas we heard about what would exclude people from receiving God's grace. All the answers were not the same, although I was surprised at how similar they were. Christianity is not unique in being a religion of grace.

THE CHURCH AND THE SPIRIT

There are other claims about the uniqueness of Christianity: only our community, the Church, really works; only we have divine help within us to change our characters. Christian ideas about the Church as Christ's body in the world and about the indwelling Holy Spirit are special, but I think what we have heard in these conversations, and what we see in practice around us, will make us wary of claiming that the other religions do not have communities that work or provide divine help towards holy living. So what shall we say about the uniqueness of Christianity?

WHAT IS UNIQUE ABOUT CHRISTIANITY?

Brother Angelo, the Franciscan friar, summed it up for me when he said, 'Christianity has got Jesus Christ and the others haven't.' These conversations have impressed upon me that it is not our personal beliefs, as members of one particular branch of the Christian religion, our assessment of the human problem, our perception of another dimension of being, our method of reaching out and finding it, our hope for more authentic satisfying lives, that mark out the Christian religion as a unique phenomenon in the world. As we have seen, similar beliefs, perceptions and hopes weave their way through the other religions too. What marks us out from these other religions is our story. We have Jesus Christ, and closely connected with that we have a community with a ritual that brings the story alive for us—the eucharist.

This story and this ritual are embedded in the whole story of the Bible and the whole practice of the Church. We use them to image, to experience, to take hold of the divine, to inform and strengthen us and to bind us together—it is these that make our religion unique.

What a story we have! What a stunning revelation it is of the real nature of God! What a sense of our own value and our own needs, what a remarkable combination of humility and confidence and inspiration to holy living this story, and this ritual, evoke! It is a story of what God has done. This is the uniqueness of Christianity. This is the story, and this is the community in which we celebrate it, that can, if we let them, transform our lives and being. This is the story we have to tell the world.[34]

A UNIVERSAL AND INCLUSIVE STORY

We have discovered, through listening to these conversations, that other people have different stories to tell and different rituals to make those stories come alive. These, in a similar way, mediate between them and the transcendent—help them image and relate to this spiritual world that we all believe lies behind the material one. This is basically what we mean when we say that they follow other religions. As we saw, many of them are as eager to share their stories as we are, and this confronts us with the fact of plurality. How are we going to react to this fact? Is there one God for the Western world and one for the Eastern? Did Jesus die only for some of the human race?

One of the things that has remained strongly in my mind is that it was the perception of the early Church, if at first a reluctant and contested one, that this story of what God had done in Jesus was a story for the whole world. Ancient Judaism had at times become rather exclusive, but the monotheism of the Old Testament was based from the beginning on the idea that there was one creator who had plans for the whole of his creation. God's promise to Abraham (Genesis 12:3) and the visions of the prophets (for example, Isaiah 2:1–3; 25:6–8) confirm this.

The New Testament carries on the idea of one God, holding the whole of humankind responsible for the way it reacts to him as its creator (and having enough evidence to have no excuse). Paul told the polytheists in Athens that the one God, who made the world and everything in it, set people here so that they would seek him, 'and perhaps reach out for him and find him, though he is not far from each one of us. "For in him we live and move and have our being"' (Acts 17:24–28).

Paul says in his letter to the Romans that God will be the judge of the whole world. 'God "will give to each person according to what he has done". To those who by persistence in doing good seek glory, honour and immortality, he will give eternal life. But for those who are self-seeking and who reject the truth and follow evil, there will be wrath and anger... For God does not show favouritism' (Romans 2:6–11).

Not only was the early Church sure about the one God, who was the creator, and judge of his whole creation, it believed that the sacrifice of Jesus was for the whole world too. Paul says, 'God was reconciling the world to himself in Christ' (2 Corinthians 5:19) and perhaps more tellingly, in his letter to Timothy, 'This is a trust-worthy saying that deserves full acceptance (and for this we labour and strive), that we have put our hope in the living God, who is the Saviour of all (people), and especially of those who believe' (1 Timothy 4:9–10). John says, 'He is the atoning sacrifice for our sins, and not only for ours but also for the sins of the whole world' (1 John 2:2).

This idea of God being the creator, judge and saviour of the whole world culminates, in the book of Revelation, in the vision of people from every nation, tribe, people and language worshipping before the throne of God and of the Lamb (Revelation 7:9).

The Christianity of the Bible is a universal religion. It is amazing how much energy of Christians through the ages has been taken up in working out whom they can exclude from this wonderfully inclusive offer of grace.

IS CHRISTIANITY EXCLUSIVE?

Some verses in the Bible have been taken, by some people, to be saying that there are those, perhaps the majority of humankind, who will ultimately be excluded from God's offer of grace. This implies that God's plan to save the human race has only been at best a qualified success, but also that of the people I interviewed who said they were depending on God's grace, some will discover that they have been misled. While they may be correct that the only way to find salvation is to seek God's grace with a humble heart, that grace is not for them. I find this idea at odds with the God of the Bible. As several of our participants (Nitin, Tom and Radha) commented, whatever Jesus meant when he said he was the only way, he couldn't have meant that.

This realization has sent me back to the Bible to look at these passages again. It's hard, when translators, commentators and preachers have assumed a certain interpretation for a long time, to see things in a different way, but one of the keys to interpretation is to see the passages in their context.

Jesus' words, 'I am the way, the truth and the life. No one comes to the Father except through me', were spoken to his closest disciples on the night before he died. A sense of gloom hung over the temple-based religion of these first-century Jews, living under the unwelcome occupation of the Romans. The story of the cross, where Jesus would make an ultimate 'full, perfect and sufficient sacrifice for the sins of the whole world'[35] was about to unfold. For them, Jesus and this remarkable act of self-giving love—marking, for those who believed in it, the end of the need for temple sacrifices—was the only way forward.

In Revelation 13:8 Jesus is described as 'the Lamb that was slain from the creation of the world'. To me, this opens up this story of the cross as an eternal, universal story that reveals what God is like, for every person, in every time and every place.

In the book of Acts, Peter is speaking to the rulers, elders and teachers of the law in Jerusalem when he says, 'Salvation is found in no one else, for there is no other name under heaven given to men by which we must be saved' (Acts 4:12). This was again in the context of an ancient form of Judaism that was going to come to an abrupt end in around 40 years' time, an event that Jesus had foreseen. It was also in the context of the surrounding Greek and Roman religions, which were both polytheistic and amoral.

It was the experience of other monotheistic and ethical religions —people of faith who seem to know and trust the one God and, in approaching him, see the need to change their way of life—that sent me back to these passages to re-examine them and see how they might be interpreted in the light of what I had heard.

IS TRUTH IN RELIGION IMPORTANT?

Although several of the people I interviewed said they believed that, in essence, or at some fundamental level, all religions teach the same things, and although this takes so much pressure off us in trying to reach an understanding with people of other faiths, I find that I am not personally able to take this way out. As other people said, it can make us complacent about finding the truth and about sharing our own story.

These conversations highlighted quite strongly to me the fact that, although there is much in common, all religions do not say the same thing about how to find a more authentic and satisfying way to live as a human being. If we are going to use the word 'truth' in a way that retains its usefulness as a concept, it must relate to how things are—just what is the case. If reincarnation is the case, in the sense that there is a causal moral connection between a succession of human beings, then the Semitic idea that each individual is responsible for only one life is not true. If the widely held view in both Eastern and Semitic religions that there is a supreme being who created the world (or who periodically recreates it) is true, then the Buddhist idea that, although there is a moral law, there is no creator, no lawgiver and no judge, is not. It may be that the two sides are misunderstanding each other or using words in a different way, but taking a relativist view of truth in religion (saying that, if we are talking about religious faith, two people can believe incompatible things and both be right) to my mind devalues the word 'truth' in this context. It appears to imply that neither are right or wrong because there is no independent reality that this language describes.

There are other ways of thinking about language that can help us, however. Some philosophers, thinking about the nature and limits of language,[36] have proposed that language is a very inefficient tool for taking hold even of the facts in the material world. As a way of helping us function as a community, it is absolutely fine but, since it can be so imprecise, since it is always changing, and since, to a large extent, it determines what we see and how we think, it never seems to get as complete a hold on 'how things are' as we would like it to.

When we are talking about God, the problem just grows. Because we can only use the words we have learnt in other contexts, all theology becomes metaphor[37] and analogy. Our words are even more slippery and ineffective in getting hold of the truth about God.

Since most Christians hold a view of scripture that is not a matter of dictation, but of co-operation, the implication must be that God is to some extent constrained by the fact that anything he wants to say to us has to be embodied in human forms of thought at a particular time and place. It has to be received and recorded within the languages we use, with all their built-in limitations, presuppositions and prejudices.

The Bible suggests that we do not know God as he is, in himself. We only know him as 'the Word', as he reveals himself to us (see, for example, John 1). As the apostle Paul put it, 'We see but a poor reflection… Now I know in part; then I shall know fully' (1 Corinthians 13:12). The Bible reveals that there is a God who is there, but we all perceive him dimly. One reason for this is the fact that our theological language, however refined it becomes, is just inadequate for the task. It may be the case that some Christians are too confident that their words can appropriate and contain God. Perhaps what we need is to return to the idea that stories and rituals actually have a better grasp on the truth about God than do creeds and faith statements. Perhaps we might go as far as to suggest that no one story could possibly say it all.

IS OUR STORY THE BEST?

Perhaps the question that is on your mind now is, 'Yes, but is our story the best?' From where I'm standing, the story of Jesus does certainly seem to be so. That is what I mean when I say that I'm a Christian. This story works for me. I have made a commitment to it. It is the story I embrace and live by and allow to define my life and being. If I didn't think that in it I find the truth about God and how to find him, or if I thought there was a better story, I wouldn't continue to do that.

I do not therefore imagine, however, that I have got God completely sewn up. Nor do I feel I have to rubbish other people's stories by declaring them wrong or faulty, incomplete or useless.

I don't know the whole truth about God as he is, and I don't know how things look from where they are standing.

CHAPTER 13

WHERE ARE WE GOING?

My husband and I like to go hill-walking when we have the time, and Wales is one of our favourite destinations. One morning we were planning to conquer the Sugar Loaf Mountain near Crickhowell with some friends. After a good breakfast we set off confidently under low clouds, but as the path began to rise, the mist began to gather and before long we were surrounded by a swirling whiteness that obscured any view, even of the path in front of us. It was confusing: following a map requires you to know where you are, as well as where you are going, and we could see neither. We kept going as best we could and about an hour later we were suddenly out of the mist. We could see above us a blue sky and the outline of the mountain top, and below us the valley still hidden by a thick layer of mist.

Our journey as Christians can sometimes feel like that. Staying where we are in the valley can seem a good option, but new challenges present themselves. I believe the Spirit is calling the Church in the Western world, in this new century, to think through its relationship with the other world faiths, and I'm hoping this book might help you to take part in the process. Questioning long-held views can make you feel as though you are being enveloped in mist—the feeling that you don't even know where you are, let alone where you are going. To some extent I still feel like that, even though I have been thinking about this subject for quite a long time. Where will this expedition lead us? Not, this side of death, I fear, to a clear definitive vision of how things are, but perhaps to a way of thinking that is faithful to scripture and obedient to the

Spirit's leading, that we can settle with and work from, and that can bring more understanding, more peace and tolerance into the world.

It might help us to start by thinking through the range of views that people have about those who hold different beliefs, most of which we have heard expressed in different ways in the conversations in this book. I am going to try to categorize these *views*, but what I found most interesting is that *people* don't fall into neat categories. Many of the things they say are said in particular contexts or qualified later by some other ideas or comments.

THE ONLY WAY

At one end of the spectrum, as you might see it, we have heard people argue that being committed to the truth of their own beliefs must involve accepting that people who believe something different are, at some level, wrong. They would argue that believing that one's own revelation is from God must involve accepting that other claims to sources of truth or other ways of finding God are corrupted or misguided.

The Greek Orthodox Christian I spoke to said, for example, that what he believed to be the truth for him must be the truth for everyone. 'I mean,' he said, 'if I didn't believe that, I wouldn't believe my own religion.' He couldn't accept that God had manufactured himself in different ways in different cultures. For him, 'Christ is God, full stop.' One of the Muslims also said that they did not claim to be exclusive truth-holders but that 'because this is the last revelation, it supersedes the others'. 'As far as belief is concerned,' another of the Muslims said, 'there can't be any wavering. If you think you have the opportunity to go to heaven and others are not going to heaven, you have a duty to tell them.'

Others expressed the same certainty about the truth of their own faith, but did not want to press the idea that this excluded the truth and value of different beliefs. The Jewish Rabbi said he believed

Judaism to be 'deeply true'. At the same time he could respect and value other paths. He told me, 'I don't believe Judaism represents the Truth in a totally exclusive manner, in such a way that we are compelled to feel that people following other paths are wrong.' One of the Buddhists said, 'For me the *Dhamma* represents the truth. I've no doubt about that at all, but I couldn't expect everybody else would think and feel the same way.'

Christians who want to express what you might call exclusivist views about other faiths would emphasize some of the texts we looked at in the last chapter.[38] They might argue that since sin is the problem that stands between people and God, and Jesus' death on the cross is the way God chose to deal with it, putting our faith in this unique event is the only way to find reconciliation with him. As we saw in the last chapter, however, this is not a view that is supported by the whole of scripture, nor by the traditions of the Churches. Roman Catholic doctrine includes the idea of the baptism of desire, and Reformation theology the idea of uncovenanted mercy.[39]

NOT THE ONLY BUT THE BEST

Some said that although their way to God might not be the only possible way, it was the best, and not just the best for them. They believed their faith was in some way objectively superior to the others, by being the quickest, easiest or surest way to God. The Sikh student I spoke to admitted that she might be biased, but said she thought Sikhism was an easier way to God than any other religion. The Hindu monk said he didn't see the Hare Krishna way as the only way, but he was confident it was 'the fastest way to get back to God'.

One of the other Hindus, however, said he wondered, when we say our belief is superior to everybody else's, 'to what degree ego is coming into this, one's pride', and another Sikh said he thought it was rather sad 'when people try to justify their own faith by downgrading other faiths'.

Christians wanting to express an inclusivist view like this might claim that while other revelations may contain some truths and have some value, the revelation of God in Jesus is somehow normative or definitive, somehow a better revelation than any other. They may want to claim that Jesus' death on the cross is central to God's provision of salvation, but recognize at the same time the possibility that people can come to benefit from what Jesus did without knowing about it or being aware of it. They would hold that God's Spirit can be active in the context of other religions, drawing people into a saving relationship with God, but want to add that, in the end, this will depend on what Jesus has done.

They could find plenty of evidence for this sort of view from the Bible. We saw before how Jesus and Paul clearly thought of Old Testament saints and Gentiles as having received God's salvation, but there are a host of other verses that make the same claim.[40]

Brother Anthony may have been expressing an inclusivist view like this in his suggestion that when Jesus said he was the only way, he didn't mean that unless you became a Christian you were doomed to eternal hellfire. He meant rather, 'Because of what I've done, because of who I am, I've opened the way for you to come.'

SEVERAL DIFFERENT WAYS

Quite a step from this is the idea that there could be more than one stream of genuine revelation or apprehension of the truth about how the world is. People might believe that God has revealed the truth about himself to (or that the true nature of the spiritual world has been grasped by) different people in different cultural situations.

In the first conversation, we heard a Hindu say, 'If the Lord had wanted to have just one faith in the world he would have fixed it. I think he did what he did because he wanted to do it… He accepts everyone's uniqueness and difference.' One of the Sikhs also believed that God had created diversity and added, 'He did it because he was so great... Every place had a different prophet... all sent by the Almighty.' I also learnt that the Qur'an teaches that God did not leave the human race alone—'There were messengers in every single locality on earth'—although I don't think any of the Muslims I spoke to would want to endorse any sort of pluralism.

Christians who do want to take a pluralist view might say that while they, and many other people across the world, have been finding God and experiencing his salvation through the story of our scriptures and through our saviour, other people have been finding him through other streams of revelation and other human figures. They would take up the argument outlined in the last chapter, about people whom you might call god-fearers, who turn up right through the Bible, and they might turn also to passages like Romans 1 and 2 and Acts 10.

ALL THE WAYS ARE THE SAME

At the other end of the spectrum, several people told me that they believed that, at some level, all religions say the same thing, point to the same goal or teach the same way. One of the Sikhs I spoke to said, for example, 'You have come to a person who believes that all religions are the same. Personally I feel there is no difference in any of them.'

This feeling that we are really all the same has inspired attempts to bring together the common elements of all these world faiths and make an amalgamated faith, rather like the attempt in the 19th century to make up an artificial common language, which was called Esperanto. The Bahai religion, that arose out of an Islamic movement in the 17th century, is one attempt to do this. It has no authoritative scriptures and no formal, public rituals. Some Christians today, in the same spirit, attempt to construct worship services, in different contexts, in which people of any faith can participate. They do this by eliminating all Christian symbols, references to Jesus or use of biblical material.

For a long while I have thought that this sort of syncretism, while based in the first place on a rather shaky optimism, destroys the very things that give religions their power. For it is the stories and rituals of our religions that enable us to think about and relate to the divine, that give content and spice to our theology and our worship and enable us to express our sense of identity and values. It does, to my mind, seriously diminish both the stature of Jesus and the motivation to talk about him.

WHERE DO WE GO FROM HERE?

The road ahead can look very misty and unclear but I feel that as people in the world become more aware of the plurality of faiths around them, and of the nature of those faiths, Christians need to take up the challenge of pressing on through this subject and seeing where we end up.

Some Christians have concluded already that any position is un-acceptable that allows the possibility of there being other genuine revelations or religious figures with privileged access to the truth about God, because they believe it is destructive of our worship, our view of the Bible and Church tradition, it diminishes the stature of Jesus and it destroys the impetus for evangelism.[41] My experience of talking to people of other faiths has led me to believe that this means shutting the door too early: I hope that we might be able to work through to some new way of thinking that does recognize the validity of other revelations and other ways to God, but does not destroy our faith in any of these ways. Let me share with you some of my thoughts.

THE LANGUAGE OF WORSHIP

It seems to me that it is possible, in the language of worship, to praise and extol Jesus as the saviour of the world, and to see him as a figure of universal, cosmic significance, the truth about whom will one day be seen and acknowledged by all created beings, without having to say that he is the only figure who has this sort of significance. In the opening to his Gospel, John talks about Jesus as the 'Word become flesh'. This is a most exciting and promising idea for me. John picks up and combines several strands of Greek and Hebrew thought to tell us that there is a meaning to life (as the Greeks would say, life is essentially rational) but also that that meaning is accessible to us and that it is personal. Beyond and behind the universe there is God, who gives all life meaning, and there is God, who communicates that meaning to us. They are not, however, two Gods; they are the same. The Word—God as he communicates with his creation—is the light that shines in the darkness of human blindness about the meaning of life. It is, says John, 'the light that gives light to every [one] who comes into the world'.[42] This is the Word that 'became flesh and made his dwelling among us' in the person of Jesus. Christians worship Jesus as the Word of God here with us, but this Word, it seems to me from this chapter, has from the beginning been the light shining in the darkness for every member of the human race.[43]

Children send cards to 'the best mum (or dad) in the world'. They use superlatives to say how much they love their parents. When Christians use such superlatives in their worship of Jesus, that seems absolutely right. This is the language of praise, of love and of gratitude. We have seen, in our conversations, that others use it too for those who have been light and life to them. This language of love and praise does not have to spill out into the denigration of other people's parents or their religions. I found the universally high esteem for Jesus, in all the conversations I had, quite remarkable.

OUR USE OF THE BIBLE AND THE TRADITIONS OF THE CHURCH

We have seen in the last two chapters that there is plenty in the Bible for us to work on. Interpretations of biblical texts are not set in stone. New situations and new ideas can send us back to the scriptures to find passages that we had not noticed or taken into account before, and to look again at the way other passages have been used in the past. Theologians and Christian philosophers from many parts of the Church are doing this work,[44] but I think I have already demonstrated that the sort of exclusiveness that is often claimed to be 'biblical' is not consistently found in the Old Testament, the Gospels or the other New Testament writings. Neither has it been consistently taught by the Church. Just as an example, from what might to some seem a rather unlikely source, the report from the Second Vatican Council of the Roman Catholic Church in 1965 stated:

Those also can attain to everlasting salvation who through no fault of their own do not know the gospel of Christ or his Church, yet sincerely seek God… Nor does divine Providence deny the help necessary for salvation to those who, without blame on their part, have not yet arrived at an explicit knowledge of God… Whatever goodness or truth is found among them is looked upon by the Church as a preparation for the gospel. She regards such qualities as given by him who enlightens all men so that they may finally have life.[45]

A BIGGER GOD; A GREATER LOVE FOR JESUS

We shall be looking at the question of evangelism, of the challenge to talk about Jesus today, in the final chapter, but I would like to share with you more of my own experiences over the period of these conversations—my own journey through the mist. I have not come through it to a settled position (I think it's fine for Christians, and for teachers, to admit that they haven't got answers to everything) but I do have a vision of what it might be like on the other side.

At first, I wondered if opening myself to the possibility that God had revealed himself in some way within cultures other than, and different from, my own would diminish my faith, and damage my trust in Jesus as the saviour of the world. I have found quite the opposite, however. I can see that it might in fact enable people to worship the one creator God in a new way, to see him more clearly as a God who loves the whole of the world he has made, who takes the initiative to reveal himself to all his creatures, who goes to every length to come to them in ways that they can understand, to enlighten them as to the true meaning of their lives, and to save them from all the things that cut them off from him and from one another.

What I have discovered from these conversations is that, among human beings of many different backgrounds who reflect on their lives, there is a widespread feeling of the deep unsatisfactoriness of lives lived on a purely materialistic level, a feeling that there must be a more satisfying, more authentic way of being human. This feeling often leads to a quest to find answers to questions about the real meaning and significance of life, to look for ways of believing that one's own life is valuable. Many people from all these different backgrounds come to see, often with the help of ancient scriptures, inspiring teachers or people who they believe are in some way 'God with us', that these answers are to be found beyond the material world. They recognize that the answers are not merely theoretical but lead to experiences, a sense of contact with the spiritual realm of being.

The route to this kind of understanding and experience is connected, for almost all of them, with being able both to see right and to live right—the need for both enlightenment and holiness. It appears that people need sources of revelation and models to inspire them: they need communities with stories and rituals to help them take hold of the truth and overcome the ego—the selfish, isolated, materialistic life. Within these communities they are able to find meaning, significance and satisfaction through living in harmony with other people, with themselves, with the divine and with his created world.

Could it be that underlying all of this is the grace of the Creator, taking the initiative and revealing himself in whatever ways we can understand, entering into our cultures and our lives in whatever ways we can recognize, to show us the truth about himself and the way to find him?

Could it be that this way to God, coming through so many of these conversations, is the way of grace, that in the end we find this authentic, satisfying, enduring way of living being offered as an undeserved gift? Perhaps the question that comes through some of these conversations—'Yes, but to whom does God offer this gift?'—needs turning round. He offers it to all, but who is ready to receive it? Again the answer comes through so much of what I have heard: it is those who have overcome the ego, found ways of transcending naturally selfish, proud and isolated ways of being, who have learned to live openly, generously, compassionately, learned in fact the secret of giving and receiving grace.

If this were the case, would it not make God immensely more worthy of praise for his compassion and his justice, his power and his victory? Would it not make the story of Jesus more moving and more inspiring, and make us more eager to share it with the rest of the world? For, if this is true, this is a brilliant story. Set up for us, as it is, by the long tale of the Old Testament about sin and sacrifice and atonement, this story is of God loving the world so much and, knowing what it will cost, being prepared to come, to convince us that our failures can be forgiven, our hurts healed—to show us just how liberating and powerfully effective it is to take the way of love rather than the way of hate, even if it also turns out to be the way of suffering.

This way of seeing things enables us to be enthusiastic about our own faith and at the same time to respect and value the stories of others, for they may have different insights that can enrich our understanding and inspire our growth in holiness. This is the way of seeing things that will enable us to recognize and celebrate the differences between people that God has created—just because he is so great.

CHAPTER 14

THE CHALLENGE TO TALK
ABOUT JESUS, AND HOW TO DO IT

I wonder if, as you read through these interviews, you ever felt frustrated that I didn't break in to the conversation to talk about Jesus. When Gurcharan Singh said he had told the visiting Christian evangelist that he would become a Christian if he could hear what it had to offer him, or when Basma Elshayyal told me that, since she was a Muslim, she believed in God's prophets and God's books so she automatically believed in Jesus and the New Testament, were you imagining what you would say next, if it were you sitting there? I often wanted to take control of the conversation and move it down a different course, but listening is a disciplined business that is important to practise, and the time comes when we do have the opportunity to speak.

A few of these conversations went on after the recording had ended, and some people did ask me then more about my own faith. I often think of the verse in one of Peter's letters, 'Always be prepared to give an answer to everyone who asks you to give the reason for the hope that you have. But do this with gentleness and respect, keeping a clear conscience' (1 Peter 3:15–16).

One response to living in a religiously plural society is to retreat behind the idea that all religions say the same thing or lead to the same goal, or are equally true or valuable or whatever. 'At the end of the day,' people have said to me, 'we all worship the same God, don't we?' If these ideas are an expression of our respect for other people's beliefs, that is fine (although, as we have seen, all religions don't say the same thing or have the same ideas about our eventual destination, and some people may be insulted by the suggestion that they do). If they are an excuse for keeping off the subject of religion in all our dealings with people who don't believe the same as we do, however, then I think that is a pity. I have found that people today are much more interested and open about what you might call the spiritual side of life than they were fifty years ago. It was then, in some circles, considered bad manners to talk about religion or politics at dinner, but today there is a very different spirit. Talking about faith, in the right way, can be very stimulating and enjoyable for all sorts of people.

It's a pity because the encouragement to 'go and tell' has, from the very beginning, been an essential aspect of the good news of Jesus. Matthew ends his Gospel with an account of Jesus' return to heaven, where he leaves his disciples with a job to do: 'Go and make disciples of all nations!' (Matthew 28:19–20). Luke, in Acts 1:8, records a similar commission: 'You will receive power when the Holy Spirit comes on you; and you will be my witnesses in Jerusalem, and in all Judea and Samaria, and to the ends of the earth.' So the first reason why, as disciples of Jesus, we should talk about him in the world today is that he told us to. We also have the example of Paul and the other apostles, who set off with courage and enthusiasm to do what they had been told.

A third reason for talking about Jesus is one that we have in common with several of the people I spoke to—the very human desire to share good news. There are people around us who suffer from meaninglessness, hopelessness and anxiety, loneliness and boredom. If we have found purpose and hope, peace and fellowship by being part of a Christian community, it would be strangely selfish not to share this fact with our friends and colleagues, whatever their background. I find that other people are eager to share the remedies to life's ills that they have found, whether it's homeopathy, living in Spain, choral singing or joining a chess club. In the end, of course, religion is not just another lifestyle option. Our commitment to the fact that our religious beliefs do actually reflect the truth about how the world is may be just the sort of rock some people are looking for.

The two verses from Charles Wesley's great hymn, 'Jesus, the name high over all', quoted at the beginning of this book, sum up for me the Christian impetus to 'go and tell'.

> *Oh, that the world might taste and see*
> *the riches of his grace!*
> *The arms of love that compass me*
> *would all mankind embrace.*
> *Happy if with my latest breath*
> *I may but gasp his name:*
> *preach him to all, and cry in death,*
> *'Behold, behold the Lamb!'*

Did you notice, though, how some aspects of the history of Christian mission were scorned and rejected by several of the people I interviewed—how they criticized the whole notion of conversion as implying an insensitive, superior and intolerant approach? How are we going to meet and talk with people who feel like this?

Clearly I don't have all the answers, but here are some thoughts that come out of my experiences over the last few months. In a way, they are relevant not just when we are talking with people who follow other faiths but when we are talking about Jesus to anyone in today's world who has not had the experience of looking at the world from where we stand.

NOT MAKING ASSUMPTIONS

First, I have learnt not to make assumptions. It is so easy to categorize people by what we can see or what we know about their cultural background or lifestyle. Someone who was brought up in India may be a practising Hindu, but they may equally be a Christian, a non-turbaned Sikh, a Muslim or completely secular in their outlook on life. Just because it appears to us that someone has no religious commitment, it doesn't mean that they have no interest in or knowledge about spiritual things. We learn about people not by making assumptions but by talking with them.

EARNING THE RIGHT TO BE TOLD

Although most people would prefer to talk about themselves than listen to someone else, you still have to win the privilege of being told about what people believe and do, their personal hopes and fears. I approached quite a lot of people, asking them to help me in this project, but there were several who didn't want to talk to a stranger about such things. Without the cover of a project like mine, you earn the right to be told, by the sort of person you are, by living your religion in a way that evokes respect and trust and by being willing to make your special commitment to Christianity known. Many people in these conversations made the point that it is by living your religion, rather than by talking about it, that you interest and impress people.

HOPING TO LEARN

As we have seen throughout this book, one result of the plurality in our societies today is that people living around us have different worldviews. They are not all looking at the world from the same place. This is becoming increasingly the case as some people are brought up in secular families, communities and schools and others are brought up in families, communities and schools that look at the world from one of several different religious viewpoints. Did you, as you read these conversations, sometimes feel this sense of alienation—that although people were using words you understood, you could not imagine what it would feel like to see the world from where they were standing? If we are going to talk to each other about life, about faith and values, we have to try to cross this gap somehow, and the way to do it is to listen to each other with a willingness to learn.

Preaching, witnessing and evangelism all seem to focus on what we say, on our telling people, but if we sound to them as if we have come from another planet, no real communication will take place. To communicate, there must be listening from both sides, and listening requires genuine humility and curiosity. We have to acknowledge that we do not know all there is to know about God and that we may, as we listen, learn something of value in our own walk with him. We may find insights into the nature of God and the way of salvation that we have never thought of, that send us back to the Bible to find things we have never noticed there before. Examples for me were the fact that Paul prayed for the Ephesians 'that the eyes of your heart may be enlightened in order that you may know the hope to which he has called you' (Ephesians 1:18), which sounds interestingly like an Eastern religious goal, and that he told the Corinthians to 'run in such a way as to get the prize' (1 Corinthians 9:24), which sounds similar to what the Muslims I interviewed were saying. My approach of encouraging people to talk about how their faith works in practice in their daily lives, rather than about their religion's official beliefs and practices, is one that you might find useful too.

A conversation that could last for a few minutes or many years could start when you show a genuine interest in someone's faith, ask about the stories in their scriptures and their rituals, and then perhaps about their experiences and hopes. It can be hard in the early days not to judge or compare, not to dismiss what you hear as incomprehensible or just barmy, but the aim should be to try to imagine what it would feel like to be standing in that person's shoes.

The time may come when you can invite them to listen to your story—to come and see how the world looks from your viewpoint. Then you can talk about Jesus and what he said and did, share what this story means to you and how it has changed your life, tell them about the Eucharist and why you like to celebrate it with the local

Christian community, share your experiences and hopes as honestly as you can. If the relationship develops, you may be able to read your friend's scriptures with them and go to their place of worship and help them to read your scriptures and to worship with you.

THE AIM OF DIALOGUE

This is dialogue. While some encounters may be very brief and fleeting and others develop into long friendships, while some might be with people firmly committed to another faith and some with people with very little spiritual experience or commitment, this spirit of dialogue, of listening to each other, is the best way to talk about Jesus in the world today, and we have a good precedent for it in Acts 17.

So what is the aim of dialogue? Is it what people call 'syncretism', which would involve giving up our differences, our different stories and rituals, and finding a common faith that merges the best of the beliefs and practices of all the participants? For me, as I suggested earlier, this in fact destroys religions. I think we saw in these conversations that it is the different stories and rituals that have the power to mediate the transcendent to us, that enable us to experience, to worship and find inspiration and strength to live well. It is precisely our differences that we want to hold on to, to celebrate and to share, to learn from.

Is the aim of dialogue that the people we engage with should convert to our religion? It has never really been *our* task to convert people. It is the Spirit of God who opens people's minds and draws them into a saving relationship with him. Our task, whether through preaching or service, has always been to create a situation, an atmosphere, in which God's Spirit can work, widening understanding and deepening faith. Dialogue seems to me an ideal situation in which that can happen, but we should never assume that the Spirit will only use these situations for the benefit of one participant in the conversation.

Our aim, then, is to share our stories, to invite others to come and stand by us and see how the world looks from here. What the writing of this book has done for me is to widen my expectations of what might then happen. God has worked, and perhaps is working, in his world today in unexpected ways.

1   From the Communion Service, *Common Worship*, Church House Publishing (2000).
2   David Lodge, *How Far Can You Go?*, Penguin, 1981, p. 113.
3   John Robinson, *Honest to God*, SCM Press, 1963, p. 7.
4   UCCF, 1988.
5   M. Juergensmeyer, 'Why religious nationalists are not fundamentalists', *Religion* Vol. 23, January, pp. 85–92, 1993.
6   Thomas Hobbes (1588–1679), *Leviathan*, (1651) Pt. ii, ch. 19.
7   Sidgwick & Jackson, 1985.
8   Nuala Ni Dhomhnaill, 'Aubade', (trs. Michael Longley), From *An Dealg Droighinn*, Mercia Press, 1981.
9   These are calculated from some statistics in Ninian Smart (ed.), *Atlas of World Religions*, Oxford University Press, 1999.
10 This is the magazine of the Jehovah's Witnesses.
11 One kind of dualism is the idea that there are two distinct kinds of things in the universe—material things and spiritual things. This is what most theistic Hindus would believe. Non-dualistic Hinduism denies this by arguing that material things are ultimately unreal.
12 To have a kosher kitchen is only to eat food permitted in the rabbinic laws and prepared in ways laid down by them.
13 *Darkenu: the Masorti Vision* (2002), The Assembly of Masorti Synagogues, 1097 Finchley Road, London NW11 OPU.
14 *Darkenu*, p. 5
15 *Darkenu*, p. 9.
16 *Darkenu*, p. 15.
17 *Nibbana* (in Pali), *Nirvana* (in Sanscrit), literally the blowing out of the fires of greed, hatred and delusion that keep one in the round of rebirth.
18 *Dhamma* (in Pali), *Dharma* (in Sanskrit). This is the teaching of the Buddha, which explains how things are. The Sangha is the community.
19 Lama Thubten Yeshe was one of the founders of the Foundation for the Preservation of the Mahayana Tradition, set up in 1975 to make the practice of Tibetan Buddhism available in the West.
20 Sangharakshita (b. 1925) founded The Friends of the Western Buddhist Order in England in 1967.
21 The Dhammapada is one of the books in the Pali canon, consisting of sayings of the Buddha.
22 Siddhartha Gotama (in Pali) or Gautama (in Sanskrit) is the human figure who lived in the fifth and fourth centuries and became known as The Buddha after his enlightenment.
23 In 1054CE the Eastern Orthodox Church split from the Roman Catholic Church, ostensibly over a dispute about the wording of the Nicene creed. The Western Church wanted to add the words 'and the Son' after the phrase 'The Holy Spirit proceeds from the Father'. The Eastern Church saw the Spirit as proceeding *from* the Father *through* the Son.
24 The Arabic word *Hadith* is often used for these collections of remembered words and actions of Muhammad and other early Muslim saints.
25 Eid Al Fitr is the celebration at the end of Ramadan, the month of fasting.
26 *Da'wa* is often translated as 'mission'.
27 *Sunnah* literally means 'way'. For Muslims it is another word for the practice of the prophet Muhammad.
28 The book is also known as the Guru Granth Sahib.

29 The five visible symbols of the Sikh faith are uncut hair and beard, a comb, a steel wristband, short under-trousers, and the sword—usually now a small ceremonial dagger.

30 Mark 9:4; 12:26–27; Luke 16:22.

31 Genesis 14:18; Romans 4:3; Exodus 18:1–27; Numbers 23—24; Hebrews 11:31; Matthew 2:1–2; 8:1–13; Acts 10:1–7.

32 If you are interested in finding out more about the concept of grace within Eastern religions, it is discussed by S.J. Samartha in *Living Faiths and Ultimate Goals*, World Council of Churches, 1974, pp. 2–11.

33 Matthew 5:1–8; 6:12–15; 25:14–15, 31–46; John 15:5–6.

34 By 'story' I simply mean a narrative way of using language rather than, say, a propositional one, which makes statements. Stories and statements of fact can relate to the truth—to how things actually are and to what actually happened—in many different ways.

35 Book of Common Prayer Communion Service.

36 David Pears' book, *Wittgenstein* (Fontana, 1971) would be one way of exploring these ideas if you are interested.

37 Sallie McFague's *Metaphorical Theology* (SCM Press, 1983) would be useful here.

38 John 14:6; Acts 4:12; 2 Timothy 5:12; 1 John 5:12.

39 The baptism of desire teaches that, in some circumstances, if you desire to be baptized but are prevented from receiving the sacrament, it can count as if you are baptized. Uncovenanted mercy is the mercy God offers to those who are not in the new covenant, just as he offered it to some who were not in the old one.

40 For example, 1 Corinthians 10:4; Romans 5:18 or 1 Timothy 4:10.

41 You can see an argument like this in Chris Wright's *The Uniqueness of Jesus*, SCM Press, 1987.

42 This is an alternative translation of verse 9, found in a footnote in the New International Version, although it is the standard in most other translations.

43 You could, if you were interested in pursuing this idea, read the theophany of Krishna in chapter 11 of the Bhagavad Gita.

44 Keith Ward's four books, *Religion and Revelation* (1994), *Religion and Creation* (1996), *Religion and Human Nature* (1998) and *Religion and Community* (1999), all published by Oxford University Press, are an example of this sort of work.

45 *Lumens Gentium* II. 16.

FURTHER READING

For a quick reference book to people, dates and ideas, the Penguin *Dictionary of Religion*, John Hinnells (ed.), Penguin, 1984, is great.

For a comprehensive, but perhaps rather old and dull, introduction to other faiths you could try the *Hutchinson Encyclopedia of Living Faiths*, R.C. Zaehner (ed.), Hutchinsons, 1958.

The *Atlas of the World's Religions*, Ninian Smart (ed.), Oxford University Press, 1999, is a wonderfully visual and imaginatively presented collection of historical and contemporary facts and figures, but it is rather expensive.

In *Six World Faiths*, W. Owen Cole (ed.), Continuum, 2002, leaders from these six world religions talk about their beliefs and practices. The chapter on Buddhism is written by Anil Goonewardene, one of the people I spoke to for this book.

For a discussion of Christian attitudes towards people of other faiths, you can find a conservative approach in *The Uniqueness of Jesus*, Chris Wright, Monarch, 2001, and a selection of liberal approaches in *The Myth of Christ's Uniqueness*, John Hick and Paul Knitter (eds.), SCM Press, 1988. Keith Ward's series of books on comparative theology, *Religion and Revelation* (1994), *Religion and Creation* (1996), *Religion and Human Nature* (1998), and *Religion and Community* (1999), Clarenden Press, is immensely stimulating if you like your reading deep and long.